QUICK AND EASY TREATS FOR CHEATS

By

Carolyn Humphries

foulsham
LONDON • NEW YORK • TORONTO • SYDNEY

foulsham

The Publishing House, Bennetts Close,
Cippenham, Berkshire, SL1 5AP, England.

ISBN 0-572-02213-1

Copyright © 1996 W. Foulsham & Co. Ltd

Cover photograph © Food Features

Printed in Great Britain by
Cox & Wyman Ltd, Reading, Berkshire.

CONTENTS

Introduction

How many times have you been to a dinner party and *known* that everything you had came from M&S or Sainsbury's? It's not the same as having something made especially for you, is it? But if you're up to your neck in work or running a home and family, or don't feel your culinary skills are up to much, there's no time – nor inclination – to shop and cook for elaborate meals. And for every day, more and more of us are having to turn to convenience foods to save time. But they can be pretty boring.

Not any more! My plan was to create a range of delectable dishes for every occasion which could all be prepared in next to no time, with the minimum of effort, from ingredients that are always at hand – if you keep a well-stocked pantry (page 5). The result is a book absolutely brimming full of exciting ideas from light-as-air soufflés to sumptuous, sinful desserts. They're all made from cans, packets and some basic frozen foods, so you will always be able to make mouthwatering meals *just like that*. And no one will know you haven't spent hours slaving over a hot stove and gone to enormous expense ... unless you tell them.

NOTES ON RECIPES

* Use either metric, Imperial or American measures for a recipe, not a combination.

* All spoon measures are level: 1 tsp = 5 ml
                                1 tbsp = 15 ml

* Eggs are size 3 unless otherwise stated.

* Wash, dry and peel where necessary, all fresh produce before preparation unless otherwise stated.

* Preheat the oven and cook on centre shelf unless otherwise stated.

* Most of the herbs used in this book are dried, for quickness. The exception is parsley. DO NOT try and substitute dried parsley for fresh, it just won't taste right. Instead, keep a bag of fresh parsley in the freezer then use from frozen as required.

* All preparation and cooking times at end of recipes are approximate and cooking time refers to conventional cooking. If a microwave or pressure cooker is used instead (as sometimes suggested), then the times will be reduced considerably.

THE WELL-STOCKED PANTRY

If you keep the following in your kitchen, you'll always be able to create a meal in a moment. These are not the only ingredients used in the book, but they form the basis of many delicious dishes. And as you discover new recipes you like, add those ingredients to your store.

TASTE TICKLERS

* Tube of tomato purée (paste)

* Jar of passata (sieved tomatoes)

* Dried herbs: mixed essential, PLUS mint, oregano, rosemary, basil, thyme, bay leaves and dill (dill weed) preferably

* Garlic powder, granules or tube of purée

* Coarse ground black pepper

* Salt (I use a low sodium variety)

* Mustard – Dijon if only keeping one

* Vinegar – red wine, white wine or cider (no need for malt as well unless you prefer it)

* Stock cubes – vegetable essential, PLUS chicken and beef preferably

* Spices – nutmeg, cinnamon, paprika, chilli or cayenne

* Curry paste or powder

* Redcurrant jelly (clear conserve)

* Sunflower oil – essential, PLUS olive oil preferably

* Sugar – caster (superfine) essential, PLUS light brown

* Dried milk (non-fat dry milk)

* Carton UHT whipping cream and/or can or frozen cream

* Lemon juice

CLEVER CANS

* Tomatoes

* Tuna

* Sweetcorn (corn)

* Red kidney beans

* Minced (ground) or stewed steak

* Ham

* Condensed soups

* Fruit in natural juice

* Custard

MAGIC MIXES

* White/cheese sauce

* Batter

* Bread sauce

* Lemon meringue pie

* Crème caramel

* Sponge cake

FRIDGE AND FREEZER FRIENDS

* Size 3 eggs
* Cheddar cheese
* Grated Parmesan cheese
* Sunflower spread (suitable for baking and spreading)
* Mayonnaise (I use a 'light' variety)
* Frozen pastry (paste): puff, filo and shortcrust (basic pie crust)
* Frozen peas
* Frozen prawns (shrimp)
* Fresh parsley (freeze in plastic bag, use from frozen)

EXCEPTIONAL EXTRAS

* Pasta – any shape
* Long-grain rice
* Plain (all-purpose) flour
* Baking powder
* Cornflour (cornstarch)
* Part-baked French sticks

VITAL VEGGIES

* Potatoes
* Onions
* Carrots
* White cabbage (to cook or shred for salad)

HELP - I'VE RUN OUT OF ...

With even the best laid plans, it's easy to run out of that vital little ingredient. Here are a few tips for alternatives you can use:

* **Tomato purée (paste)**: use ketchup (catsup), passata (sieved tomatoes), canned or packet tomato soup – you'll be amazed what a cup-a-soup can do sprinkled into a casserole!

* Wine: use 1 part wine vinegar to 2 parts water. If the result is a little sharp, add a little sugar (2.5-5 ml/½-1 tsp should be sufficient). If you have a drop of sherry, vermouth or cider, these make good substitutes for wine in recipes.

* Stock cubes – CHICKEN: 1 chicken cup-a-soup for up to 300 ml/½ pt/1¼ cups stock (chicken noodle is ideal and the noodles will cook out in the casserole) or Chicken Bovril (use sparingly)
BEEF: canned consommé is ideal, or Bovril (use sparingly), or oxtail cup-a-soup (see chicken)
VEGETABLE: Marmite or Vegimite (use sparingly), or vegetable cup-a-soup (see chicken)
ALL: Brown table sauce/Worcestershire sauce/soy sauce can add flavour and colour too.

*Flour (for thickening soups, sauces and casseroles): crumble in a Weetabix, or add a little instant oat cereal or mashed potato powder a spoonful at a time, whisking in well.

* Sugar: if your recipe calls for caster (superfine) or icing (confectioners') sugar and all you have is granulated – tip it into the food processor and grind it down. If you have white sugar and your recipe calls for brown, add 5 ml/1 tsp or so of gravy browning to the mixture (you won't get quite the same flavour, but the colour will be right!)

* Chocolate: if you need plain (semi-sweet) chocolate or cocoa (unsweetened chocolate) powder and all you have is milk chocolate or drinking (sweetened) chocolate powder, add 2.5-5 ml/½-1 tsp instant coffee dissolved in the smallest amount of water to it. If the recipe calls for milk chocolate and you have plain (semi-sweet) only, add 15-30 ml/1-2 tbsp dried milk (non-fat dry milk) powder to any dry ingredients, or blend it with the smallest amount of warm water until smooth to add to 'wet' ingredients.

* Golden (light corn) syrup: clear honey can be substituted.

* Breadcrumbs as a topping or coating: crushed cornflakes/branflakes, porridge oats or, for a savoury coating, stuffing mix can be used instead.

Soups

Hot or cold, thick or thin, a bowl of soup makes a delicious light meal or starter for a dinner party. Of course, you could just open a can – but the taste is rarely exciting. Don't settle for second best. If you are really pushed for time, try mixing a can of cream of tomato soup with a can of chopped tomatoes. Spice it up with a spoonful of Worcestershire sauce, sprinkle with crisply fried croûtons and you have a Tomato Special. This just shows you that with a little inspiration you can create masterpieces!

MINTED PEA SOUP

Serves 4	Metric	Imperial	American
Frozen peas	*225 g*	*8 oz*	*2 cups*
Vegetable or chicken stock	*600 ml*	*1 pt*	*2¹/₂ cups*
Dried mint	*5 ml*	*1 tsp*	*1 tsp*
Pepper	*pinch*	*pinch*	*pinch*
Instant mashed potato (optional to thicken)	*30 ml*	*2 tbsp*	*2 tbsp*
Single (light) cream	*150 ml*	*¹/₄ pt*	*²/₃ cup*
To garnish:			
Dried chives or dried mint			

1. Cook the peas in the stock with the mint for 5 minutes.

2. Liquidise or sieve and return to the saucepan.

3. Season with a little pepper and whisk in the potato, if using.

4. Stir in all but 30 ml/2 tbsp of the cream.

5. Reheat but DO NOT BOIL, or chill. Serve in soup bowls, garnished with a swirl of the reserved cream and a sprinkling of herbs.

Preparation time: 2 mins
Cooking time: 5 mins plus reheating or chilling time.

TANGY CARROT AND TOMATO SOUP

Serves 4	Metric	Imperial	American
Can carrots	275 g	10 oz	10 oz
Can tomatoes	400 g	14 oz	14 oz
Pure orange juice	150 ml	1/4 pt	2/3 cup
Dried basil or mixed herbs	5 ml	1 tsp	1 tsp
Salt and pepper			
To serve:			
Plain yoghurt or a little cream (any will do)	20 ml	4 tsp	4 tsp

1. Drain the carrots and place in a food processor or blender.

2. Add the contents of the can of tomatoes and blend until smooth. Alternatively, pass both through a sieve (strainer).

3. Add the orange juice, herbs and seasoning to taste.

4. Heat through or chill, and serve in bowls with 5 ml/1 tsp of yoghurt or cream spooned over each portion.

 Preparation time: 2 mins
Cooking time: 2 mins or chilling time

CRAB BISQUE

Serves 6	Metric	Imperial	American
Onion, very finely chopped	1	1	1
Butter or margarine	25 g	1 oz	2 tbsp
Can dressed crab	43 g	1¾ oz	1¾ oz
Plain (all-purpose) flour	45 ml	3 tbsp	3 tbsp
Fish, chicken or vegetable stock	900 ml	1½ pts	3¾ cups
Celery salt	5 ml	1 tsp	1 tsp
Dry sherry	30 ml	2 tbsp	2 tbsp
Milk	150 ml	¼ pt	⅔ cup
Single (light) cream	150 ml	¼ pt	⅔ cup
Can white crabmeat	170 g	6 oz	6 oz
To garnish:			
Croûtons (see Tomato Special page 13)			

1. Fry (sauté) the onion gently in the butter in a saucepan for 3 minutes until soft but not brown.

2. Stir in the dressed crab and the flour and cook for 1 minute.

3. Remove from the heat and gradually blend in the stock. Bring to the boil, stirring until thickened. Simmer for 15 minutes.

4. Stir in the remaining ingredients. Reheat but DO NOT BOIL. Serve in soup bowls garnished with croûtons.

Preparation time: 2 mins
Cooking time: 20 mins

RICH GREEN SOUP

Instead of frozen spinach and beans, you could use drained cans of beans and spinach and simmer for 5 minutes only. The result will not however be so good in colour or flavour.

Serves 6	Metric	Imperial	American
Onion, chopped	*1*	*1*	*1*
Butter or margarine	*15 g*	*½ oz*	*1 tbsp*
Frozen broad (lima) beans	*225 g*	*8 oz*	*2 cups*
Frozen chopped spinach	*225 g*	*8 oz*	*1 cup*
Vegetable or chicken stock	*900 ml*	*1½ pts*	*3¾ cups*
Grated nutmeg	*1.5 ml*	*¼ tsp*	*¼ tsp*
Salt and pepper			
To garnish:			
Crisp crumbled bacon (optional)			

1. Fry (sauté) the onion in the butter in a large saucepan for 3 minutes until soft but not brown.

2. Add the beans, spinach and stock.

3. Bring to the boil, reduce the heat, cover and simmer for 10 minutes or until beans and onion are soft.

4. Pour into a food processor or blender and process until smooth, or pass through a sieve (strainer).

5. Season to taste with nutmeg, salt and pepper. Reheat and serve with crisp, crumbled bacon sprinkled over, if liked.

Preparation time: 2 mins
Cooking time: 10 mins

CHICKEN AND CORN CHOWDER

Serves 4	Metric	Imperial	American
Can condensed cream of chicken soup	295 g	10½ oz	10½ oz
Milk			
Can sweetcorn (corn)	200 g	7 oz	7 oz
Cayenne	pinch	pinch	pinch
To garnish:			
Single (light) cream (optional)	30 ml	2 tbsp	2 tbsp
Chopped parsley			

1. Empty the soup into a saucepan. Fill the empty soup can with milk and gradually blend to it.

2. Add the contents of the can of corn and season with the cayenne.

3. Heat through gently, stirring occasionally.

4. Serve in soup bowls, garnished with a little cream, if liked, and some chopped parsley.

 Preparation time: 1 min
Cooking time: 3 mins

ITALIAN-STYLE CONSOMMÉ

Serves 4	Metric	Imperial	American
Elbow macaroni or other small soup pasta	40 g	1½ oz	⅓ cup
Salt			
Can condensed consommé	275 g	10 oz	10 oz
Red wine or port	30 ml	2 tbsp	2 tbsp
To serve:			
Grated Parmesan cheese			

1. Cook the pasta in plenty of boiling salted water until tender. Drain and rinse with hot water.

2. Empty the consommé into a saucepan. Add water as directed and heat through. Stir in the wine or port and the pasta. Reheat.

3. Ladle into soup bowls and serve with grated Parmesan cheese.

Preparation time: 2 mins
Cooking time: 10 mins

CHINESE EGG FLOWER SOUP

Serves 4	Metric	Imperial	American
Chicken stock	900 ml	1¹/₂ pts	3³/₄ cups
Soy sauce	15 ml	1 tbsp	1 tbsp
Dry sherry	30 ml	2 tbsp	2 tbsp
Ground ginger	pinch	pinch	pinch
Frozen peas	25 g	1 oz	¹/₄ cup
Egg, beaten	1	1	1
To serve:			
Prawn crackers (optional)			

1. Put all the ingredients except the egg in a saucepan and heat to boiling point.

2. Remove from the heat and pour the egg in a thin stream through the prongs of a fork, so it solidifies in 'flowers'.

3. Let it stand for 10 seconds for the egg to set, then ladle into soup bowls. Serve with prawn crackers, if liked.

Preparation time: 2 mins
Cooking time: 3 mins

SPANISH SUMMER SOUP

For convenience, red and green (bell) peppers can be frozen whole, then chopped for use as required.

Serves 4	Metric	Imperial	American
Slice white bread	1	1	1
Lemon juice	15 ml	1 tbsp	1 tbsp
Small onion, roughly chopped	1/2	1/2	1/2
Small garlic clove, crushed (optional)	1	1	1
Lettuce leaves (use the outside ones you usually discard)	4	4	4
Piece cucumber (the end will do)	5 cm	2 in	2 in
Red (bell) pepper (optional)	1/2	1/2	1/2
Olive oil	30 ml	2 tbsp	2 tbsp
Can tomatoes	400 g	14 oz	14 oz
Tomato purée (paste)	15 ml	1 tbsp	1 tbsp
Salt and pepper			
Caster (superfine) sugar	pinch	pinch	pinch
Iced water	150 ml	1/4 pt	2/3 cup
To garnish:			
Cucumber slices (optional)			

1. Soak the bread in a little water for 1 minute. Squeeze out and place in a blender or food processor with all the other ingredients, except the iced water.

2. Run the machine until the mixture is blended. Stir in the iced water and serve in soup bowls. Float a slice of cucumber on each bowl if liked.

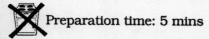 Preparation time: 5 mins

MONDAY MULLIGATAWNY

This recipe is so-called because it utilises the vegetables left over from the Sunday roast.

Serves 4	Metric	Imperial	American
Cooked leftover mixed vegetables (or frozen)	225 g	8 oz	2 cups
Garlic clove, crushed	1	1	1
Curry paste	5-10 ml	1-2 tsp	1-2 tsp
Oil	15 ml	1 tbsp	1 tbsp
Vegetable stock	600 ml	1 pt	2½ cups
Tomato purée (paste)	15 ml	1 tbsp	1 tbsp
Instant mashed potato (optional)	15 ml	1 tbsp	1 tbsp
Salt and pepper			
To garnish:			
Slices of lemon			

1. Fry (sauté) the vegetables, garlic and curry paste in the oil for 1 minute.

2. Add the stock and tomato purée, bring to the boil and simmer for 5 minutes.

3. Purée in a liquidiser or food processor. Thicken, if liked, with mashed potato and season to taste. Reheat.

4. Serve in warm soup bowls with a slice of lemon on top.

Preparation time: 2 mins
Cooking time: 7 mins

STARTERS

A starter should set the taste buds tingling in anticipation for what else is to come, so remember to keep portions small. Many of the following recipes would also make delicious light lunches served with lots of crusty bread and a side salad. And of course they're as easy to make as falling off a log! Flageolets Vinaigrette sounds delicious doesn't it. Well, simply rinse and drain a can of flageolet beans. Toss with a crushed garlic clove, 45 ml/3 tbsp of olive oil, 15 ml/1 tbsp of white wine vinegar and some thyme, parsley and seasoning and serve with crusty bread.

ARTICHOKE AND PRAWN MOSCOVA

Serves 4	Metric	Imperial	American
Can artichoke hearts	425 g	15 oz	15 oz
Frozen prawns (shrimp), thawed	175 g	6 oz	1 1/2 cups
Olive oil	45 ml	3 tbsp	3 tbsp
White wine vinegar	15 ml	1 tbsp	1 tbsp
Salt and pepper			
Soured (dairy sour) cream	150 ml	1/4 pt	2/3 cup
To garnish:			
Danish lumpfish roe			

1. Drain the artichokes and roughly chop them. Mix with the prawns.

2. Sprinkle over the oil, vinegar and a little salt and pepper and toss lightly.

3. Spoon into 4 wine goblets. Top each with a spoonful of soured cream. Chill.

4. Just before serving, top the cream with a spoonful of Danish lumpfish roe.

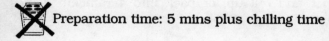 Preparation time: 5 mins plus chilling time

TUNA CHEESE

Cartons of soft cheese freeze well.

Serves 4–6	Metric	Imperial	American
Can tuna, drained	185 g	6½ oz	6½ oz
Low-fat soft cheese	200 g	7 oz	scant 1 cup
Lemon juice	15 ml	1 tbsp	1 tbsp
Cayenne	1.5 ml	¼ tsp	¼ tsp
Salt and pepper			
Chopped parsley	15 ml	1 tbsp	1 tbsp
To garnish:			
Paprika			
Lemon wedges			
Sprigs of parsley or salad leaves			
To serve:			
Hot toast			

1. Mash the tuna in a bowl with the cheese.

2. Add the remaining ingredients and mix well.

3. Either shape into a sausage on greaseproof (waxed) paper and roll up, or pack into 4 ramekin dishes (custard cups). Chill.

4. Cut the roll into 12 slices. Place the slices or ramekins on individual plates and garnish with paprika, lemon wedges and parsley or salad leaves. Serve with hot toast.

Preparation time: 5 mins plus chilling time

PILCHARD CREAMS

Serves 4	Metric	Imperial	American
Can pilchards in tomato			
sauce	*425 g*	*15 oz*	*15 oz*
Mayonnaise	*30 ml*	*2 tbsp*	*2 tbsp*
Tomato purée (paste)	*15 ml*	*1 tbsp*	*1 tbsp*
Can cream	*100 g*	*4 oz*	*4 oz*
Red wine vinegar	*5 ml*	*1 tsp*	*1 tsp*
Salt			
Cayenne	*1.5 ml*	*¹/₄ tsp*	*¹/₄ tsp*
To garnish:			
Parsley (optional)			
To serve:			
Hot toast			

1. Empty the pilchards into a bowl. Discard the bones then mash well.

2. Add the mayonnaise and tomato purée and beat well with a wooden spoon.

3. Drain the whey from the can of cream and beat into the fish with the vinegar and seasonings. Pack into ramekin dishes (custard cups) and chill, if you have time.

4. Garnish with parsley, if liked, and serve with hot toast.

Preparation time: 5 mins plus chilling time (optional)

SARDINE PÂTÉ

Serves 6	Metric	Imperial	American
Cans of sardines in oil	*2 x 125 g*	*2 x 5 oz*	*2 x 5 oz*
Butter, melted	*75 g*	*3 oz*	*¹/₃ cup*
Plain yoghurt	*150 ml*	*¹/₄ pt*	*²/₃ cup*
Lemon juice	*5 ml*	*1 tsp*	*1 tsp*
Cayenne	*1. 5 ml*	*¹/₄ tsp*	*¹/₄ tsp*
Salt and pepper			
To garnish:			
Hard-boiled (hard-cooked)			
* eggs*	*3*	*3*	*3*
Small onions, separated into			
* rings*	*2*	*2*	*2*
Chopped parsley			
To serve:			
Melba toast			

1. Drain the sardines and place in a food processor or blender with the butter, yoghurt, lemon juice and cayenne. Run the machine until smooth.

2. Add salt and pepper to taste then pack into a small pot and chill until quite firm (about 2 hours).

3. Spoon on to individual plates. Garnish with wedges of egg, onion rings and chopped parsley. Serve with melba toast.

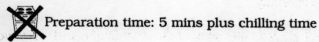 Preparation time: 5 mins plus chilling time

MARINATED KIPPER FILLETS

Make this dish in the morning and it will be ready for dinner.

Serves 6	Metric	Imperial	American
Packets frozen kipper fillets, thawed	2 x 175 g	2 x 6 oz	2 x 6 oz
Small onion, separated into rings	1	1	1
Bay leaf	1	1	1
Olive oil	90 ml	6 tbsp	6 tbsp
Red wine vinegar	30 ml	2 tbsp	2 tbsp
Dijon mustard	5 ml	1 tsp	1 tsp
Caster (superfine) sugar	1.5 ml	1/4 tsp	1/4 tsp
Salt and pepper			
To garnish:			
Parsley			
To serve:			
Brown bread and butter			

1. Pull the skin off the kipper fillets and lay the fish in a large shallow dish. Arrange the onion rings over and add bay leaf.

2. Whisk the remaining ingredients together and pour over the fish. Leave in a cool place to marinate for several hours until the fish feels tender when pierced with the point of a knife. Turn over in the marinade occasionally.

3. Remove the bay leaf. Fold the fillets and arrange decoratively on shallow individual serving dishes. Spoon the marinade and onion rings over. Garnish with parsley and serve with brown bread and butter.

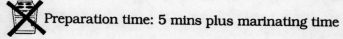 Preparation time: 5 mins plus marinating time

HAM AND PINEAPPLE COCKTAIL

Serves 6	Metric	Imperial	American
Long-grain rice	75 g	3 oz	1/3 cup
Olive oil	30 ml	2 tbsp	2 tbsp
Lemon juice	10 ml	2 tsp	2 tsp
Soy sauce	5 ml	1 tsp	1 tsp
Small onion, finely chopped	1/2	1/2	1/2
Can ham	215 g	7 1/2 oz	7 1/2 oz
Can pineapple chunks in natural juice	225 g	8 oz	8 oz
Black olives, stoned (pitted)	12	12	12
Mayonnaise	30 ml	2 tbsp	2 tbsp

1. Cook the rice in plenty of boiling salted water for 10 minutes until tender. Drain, rinse with cold water and drain again.

2. Mix the olive oil, lemon juice, soy sauce and onion together. Add to the rice, toss well and divide between 6 plates, forming a ring of rice on each plate.

3. Dice the ham, discarding any jelly. Drain the pineapple, reserving 15 ml/1 tbsp of the juice.

4. Quarter 6 of the olives and mix with the ham and pineapple.Pile into the rice rings. Mix the mayonnaise with the reserved pineapple juice and spoon a little over each. Garnish with whole olives.

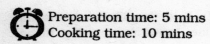

Preparation time: 5 mins
Cooking time: 10 mins

MULLED FLORIDA COCKTAIL

Serves 6	Metric	Imperial	American
Can mandarin oranges in syrup	300 g	11 oz	11 oz
Can grapefruit segments in syrup	410 g	14¹/₂ oz	14¹/₂ oz
White wine	60 ml	4 tbsp	4 tbsp
Cinnamon stick	1	1	1
Cloves	2	2	2
To garnish:			
Maraschino cherries			

1. Drain syrup from both fruits into a saucepan. Add wine, cinnamon stick and cloves. Bring to the boil, reduce heat and simmer very gently for 3 minutes.

2. Remove cinnamon and cloves, add fruit and heat through gently but do not boil.

3. Spoon into wine goblets. Top each with a maraschino cherry and serve straight away.

 Preparation time: 2 mins
Cooking time: 3 mins

SICILIAN PIMIENTOS

Serves 4–6	Metric	Imperial	American
Can whole pimientos	2 x 400 g	2 x 14 oz	2 x 14 oz
Olive oil	45 ml	3 tbsp	3 tbsp
Coarse sea salt			
To garnish:			
Black or green olives			
(optional)			
To serve:			
Ciabatta bread, hot			

1. Drain pimientos and dry on kitchen paper.

2. Heat oil in a large frying pan (skillet) and fry (sauté) pimientos for 1-2 minutes on each side until sizzling.

3. Transfer to warm serving plates, drizzle oil from pan over. Sprinkle with coarse sea salt, garnish with olives, if using, and serve straight away with hot ciabatta bread.

 Preparation time: 2 mins
Cooking time: 2-4 mins.

PEARS WITH BLUE CHEESE DRESSING

Serves 6	Metric	Imperial	American
Can pear halves	550 g	1 lb 4 oz	1 lb 4 oz
Lettuce leaves			
Dressing:			
Danish blue cheese	100 g	4 oz	1 cup
Cream, preferably double			
(heavy)	60 ml	4 tbsp	4 tbsp
Mayonnaise	45 ml	3 tbsp	3 tbsp
Lemon juice	5 ml	1 tsp	1 tsp
Milk			
To garnish:			
Paprika			

1. Drain pears and arrange fruit, rounded sides up on lettuce leaves on serving plates.

2. Mash cheese then beat in half the cream until fairly smooth.

3. Beat in remaining cream, mayonnaise and lemon juice. Thin with a little milk if necessary to give a coating consistency.

4. Spoon over pears and garnish with paprika.

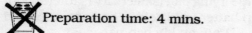 Preparation time: 4 mins.

27

CORN FRITTERS
WITH PEANUT SAUCE

Serves 6	Metric	Imperial	American
Peanut Sauce:			
Can coconut milk	300 g	11 oz	11 oz
Crunchy peanut butter	75 ml	5 tbsp	5 tbsp
Sugar	10 ml	2 tsp	2 tsp
Chilli powder	1.5 ml	1/4 tsp	1/4 tsp
Lemon juice	5 ml	1 tsp	1 tsp
Garlic clove, crushed	1	1	1
Fritters:			
Plain (all-purpose) flour	90 ml	6 tbsp	6 tbsp
Eggs	2	2	2
Milk	60 ml	4 tbsp	4 tbsp
Can sweetcorn (corn)	300 g	11 oz	1·1 oz
Salt and pepper			
Oil for frying			

1. Put all ingredients for sauce in a pan and heat through gently, stirring occasionally until sauce boils.

2. Make fritters. Put flour in a bowl. Beat eggs and milk together. Add to flour and beat well until smooth.

3. Add drained corn and a little seasoning. Mix well.

4. Heat oil in a large frying pan (skillet), fry (sauté) spoonfuls of the corn batter until golden on base, turn and fry other sides. Drain on kitchen paper.

5. Spoon sauce into 4 individual dishes on serving plates, arrange fritters around and serve hot.

 Preparation time: 5 mins
Cooking time: 10 mins

Pâté Nests

Serves 4	Metric	Imperial	American
Cases:			
Slices bread, from sliced loaf	*4*	*4*	*4*
Butter or margarine			
Filling:			
Smooth liver pâté	*100 g*	*4 oz*	*¼ lb*
Mayonnaise	*15 ml*	*1 tbsp*	*1 tbsp*
Hard-boiled (hard-cooked) egg, finely chopped	*1*	*1*	*1*
Cocktail gherkins (cornichons), finely chopped	*4*	*4*	*4*
To garnish:			
Paprika			

1. Cut crusts off bread, spread liberally with butter or margarine.

2. Press firmly into 4 sections of a tartlet tin (patty pan).

3. Bake in a moderately hot oven 190°C/375°F/gas mark 5 for about 25 minutes or until golden brown. Transfer to a wire rack to cool.

4. Make filling: mash pâté with mayonnaise. Stir in chopped egg and gherkins. Pile into bread cases and garnish with paprika.

Preparation time: 5 mins
Cooking time: 25 mins plus cooling time

MELON COCKTAIL WITH HERBY CHEESE SLICES

Serves 4–6	Metric	Imperial	American
Can melon balls	*410 g*	*14¹/₂ oz*	*14¹/₂ oz*
Can mandarin oranges	*300 g*	*11 oz*	*11 oz*
Ginger wine	*60 ml*	*4 tbsp*	*4 tbsp*
Herby Cheese Slices:			
Small French stick	*1*	*1*	*1*
Garlic and herb soft cheese	*80 g*	*3¹/₂ oz*	*3 ¹/₂ oz*
Butter or margarine	*25 g*	*1 oz*	*2 tbsp*

1. Put contents of cans of melon and mandarins into a glass bowl. Pour over ginger wine, stir then chill until ready to serve.

2. Cut French stick into 12 slices. Toast on one side under a grill (broiler). Mash soft cheese and butter or margarine together and spread over untoasted sides of bread.

3. Just before serving grill (broil) until cheese mixture is melted and bubbling. Serve straight away with the fruit cocktail.

 Preparation time: 2 mins plus chilling time
Cooking time: 5 mins

CREAMY MUSSELS

Serves 6	Metric	Imperial	American
Onion, finely chopped	*1*	*1*	*1*
Butter or margarine	*15 g*	*½ oz*	*1 tbsp*
Cans mussels in brine	*2 x 250 g*	*2 x 9 oz*	*2 x 9 oz*
White wine or dry vermouth	*150 ml*	*¼ pt*	*⅔ cup*
Water	*150 ml*	*¼ pt*	*⅔ cup*
Cornflour (cornstarch)	*15 ml*	*1 tbsp*	*1 tbsp*
Single (light) cream	*150 ml*	*¼ pt*	*⅔ cup*
Pepper			
Chopped parsley	*30 ml*	*2 tbsp*	*2 tbsp*
To serve:			
French bread			

1. Fry (sauté) onion in the butter or margarine for 2 minutes until soft but not brown.

2. Drain one of the cans of mussels and add them to the onions with the complete contents of the other can. Add the wine.

3. Blend water with the cornflour and stir in. Bring to the boil stirring until thickened.

4. Stir in the cream, some pepper to taste and chopped parsley. Heat through but DO NOT BOIL. Spoon into bowls and serve with French bread.

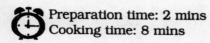 Preparation time: 2 mins
Cooking time: 8 mins

TUNA DIP

Serves 4–6	Metric	Imperial	American
Can tuna, drained	185 g	6¹/₂ oz	6 ¹/₂ oz
Mayonnaise	60 ml	4 tbsp	4 tbsp
Plain yoghurt	45 ml	3 tbsp	3 tbsp
Tomato ketchup (catsup)	15 ml	1 tbsp	1 tbsp
Lemon juice	5 ml	1 tsp	1 tsp
Chilli powder	1.5 ml	¹/₄ tsp	¹/₄ tsp
Pepper			
To serve:			
Vegetable 'dippers' OR plain crisps (potato chips) OR fingers of crisp toast			

1.   Put tuna in a bowl and break up with a wooden spoon.

2.   Beat in remaining ingredients until well blended. Turn into a small bowl and surround with vegetable 'dippers' like small florets of cauliflower, sticks of cucumber, carrot and green or red (bell) pepper, OR crisps, OR fingers of crisp toast.

 Preparation time: 3 mins plus chilling time

MIDDLE EASTERN DIP

Use other pulses like canned butter beans, flageolet or cannellini beans if you prefer.

Serves 4–6	Metric	Imperial	American
Can chick peas (garbanzo beans), drained	440 g	15¹/2 oz	15¹/2 oz
Garlic clove, crushed	1	1	1
Olive oil	90 ml	6 tbsp	6 tbsp
Lemon juice	15 ml	1 tbsp	1 tbsp
Salt and pepper			
To garnish:			
A little olive oil			
Dried mint			
To serve:			
Fingers of warm pitta bread			

1. Put chick peas and garlic in a blender or food processor and run machine until they are smooth.

2. Gradually add oil in a thin stream, keeping machine running.

3. Add lemon juice and season with salt and pepper.

4. Turn into a small bowl, drizzle a little olive oil over and sprinkle with dried mint. Serve with warm fingers of pitta bread.

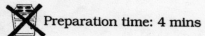 Preparation time: 4 mins

HERRING AND POTATO SALAD

Serves 6	Metric	Imperial	American
Roll-mop herrings	*4*	*4*	*4*
Can new potatoes, drained	*275 g*	*10 oz*	*10 oz*
Mayonnaise	*30 ml*	*2 tbsp*	*2 tbsp*
Plain yoghurt	*15 ml*	*1 tbsp*	*1 tbsp*
Dried dill (dill weed)	*5 ml*	*1 tsp*	*1 tsp*
Black pepper			
To garnish:			
Lettuce leaves			
A little extra dill (dill weed)			
To serve:			
Rye bread			

1. Using a sharp knife, slice each roll-mop into 6 pin-wheels.

2. Cut potatoes in quarters or sixths.

3. Mix mayonnaise, yoghurt and dill and season with pepper. Add to potatoes and toss lightly.

4. Put a small pile of potato onto lettuce leaves on each of 6 serving plates. Arrange 4 slices of roll-mop alongside attractively. Dust potato with a little more dill. Chill, if time, before serving with rye bread.

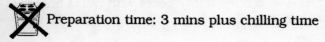 Preparation time: 3 mins plus chilling time

NUTTY CHEESE AND PINEAPPLE

This mixture can also be used to top pear or peach halves.

Serves 4	Metric	Imperial	American
Can pineapple slices	225 g	8 oz	8 oz
Cottage cheese	225 g	8 oz	1 cup
Walnut pieces, chopped	50 g	2 oz	¹/₂ cup
Grated onion	2.5 ml	¹/₂ tsp	¹/₂ tsp
Black pepper			
To garnish:			
Lettuce leaves			
Paprika			
To serve:			
Garlic bread (page 183)			

1. Drain pineapple slices and dry on kitchen paper. Arrange on lettuce leaves on 4 individual plates.

2. Mix cheese, nuts and onion together and season with a little pepper.

3. Pile into centres of pineapple rings so you can still see rim of pineapple. Dust with paprika and chill, if time, before serving with garlic bread.

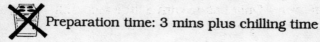 Preparation time: 3 mins plus chilling time

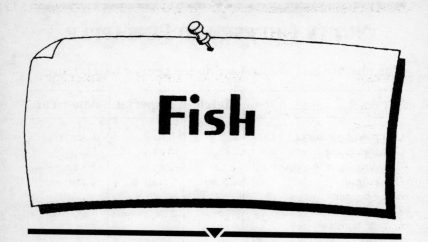

Fish

Many people are turning to fish as it is light, easily digestible and suitable for all but vegans. With so many canned and frozen varieties available, it makes the ideal choice for a quick meal. Here's a quick idea to set off you imagination. To 4 lightly fried cod steaks, add a small can of chopped tomatoes, a small can of drained green beans, 15 ml/ 1 tbsp of tomato purée, 5 ml/ 1 tsp of caster sugar and a pinch of cayenne. Heat through for 6 minutes then serve on a bed of rice: Spicy Cod with Beans.

CHEESY PRAWN SUPPER

Serves 4	Metric	Imperial	American
Frozen prawns (shrimp), thawed	225 g	8 oz	2 cups
Can condensed cream of mushroom soup	295 g	10½ oz	10½ oz
Tomato ketchup (catsup)	15 ml	1 tbsp	1 tbsp
Breadcrumbs, fresh	50 g	2 oz	1 cup
Cheddar cheese, grated	100 g	4 oz	1 cup
To serve:			
Plain boiled rice			
Toasted flaked almonds			
Broccoli			

1. Mix prawns with the soup, ketchup and half the breadcrumbs and cheese.

2. Turn into a fairly shallow ovenproof serving dish.

3. Mix remaining breadcrumbs with cheese and spoon over.

4. Bake in a hot oven 200°C/400°F/gas mark 6 for 20-25 minutes until golden and bubbling.

5. Serve with plain boiled rice garnished with toasted almonds and broccoli.

Preparation time: 3 mins
Cooking time: 20-25 mins

SMOKED MACKEREL BAKE

Serves 4	Metric	Imperial	American
Frozen or canned smoked mackerel fillets	4	4	4
Can button mushrooms	300 g	11 oz	11 oz
Packet white sauce mix	1	1	1
Milk or water (according to packet directions)	300 ml	1/2 pt	1 1/4 cups
Horseradish cream	20 ml	4 tsp	4 tsp
Cheese and onion crisps (potato chips), crushed	50 g	2 oz	1 cup
To serve:			
New potatoes			
Peas			

1. Remove skin from fish fillets, break mackerel into pieces and place in a fairly shallow ovenproof dish. Drain mushrooms and scatter over.

2. Make up sauce according to packet directions. Add horseradish.

3. Pour sauce over fish and sprinkle with crisps. Bake in a moderately hot oven 190°C/375°F/gas mark 5 for about 30 minutes or until bubbling and golden. Serve with new potatoes and peas.

 Preparation time: 3 mins
Cooking time: 30 mins

TUNA AND CORN PASTA

Serves 4	Metric	Imperial	American
Pasta shapes	225 g	8 oz	2 cups
Packet cheese sauce mix	1	1	1
Milk or water (according to directions)	300 ml	1/2 pt	1 1/4 cups
Can tuna, drained	185 g	6 1/2 oz	6 1/2 oz
Can sweetcorn (corn)	200 g	7 oz	7 oz
Cheddar cheese, grated (optional)			
To garnish:			
Chopped parsley			
To serve:			
Salad			

1. Cook pasta according to packet directions, drain.

2. Meanwhile, make up cheese sauce with milk or water according to packet directions. Add drained tuna and sweetcorn, stir and heat through.

3. Add to drained pasta and toss well. Either serve as it is sprinkled with chopped parsley or turn into a flameproof serving dish, top with a little grated cheese and brown under a hot grill (broiler) before garnishing and serving with salad.

 Preparation time: 2 mins
Cooking time: 10-12 mins

TUNA GNOCCHI

Serves 4	Metric	Imperial	American
Milk	600 ml	1 pt	2½ cups
Salt	7.5 ml	1½ tsp	1½ tsp
Pepper			
Bay leaf	1	1	1
Grated nutmeg	1.5 ml	¼ tsp	¼ tsp
Semolina (cream of wheat)	150 g	5 oz	⅔ cup
Eggs	2	2	2
Cheddar cheese, grated	100 g	4 oz	1 cup
Can tuna	185 g	6½ oz	6½ oz
Can condensed cream of mushroom soup	295 g	10½ oz	10½ oz
Butter, melted			

1. Put milk, salt, a little pepper, bay leaf, nutmeg and semolina in a pan. Bring to the boil and cook for 10 minutes, stirring until really thick. Discard bay leaf.

2. Beat in eggs and 75 g/3 oz/¾ cup of the cheese. Turn into a well-greased baking tin (pan) and smooth out with a wet palette knife to a square about 2 cm/¾ in thick. Leave to cool, then chill for 1 hour.

3. Meanwhile, drain tuna and mix with the soup. Turn into a 1.2 L/2 pt/5 cup ovenproof dish. Cut gnocchi into 4 cm/1½ in squares and arrange around top of dish. Brush with a little melted butter and sprinkle with remaining cheese.

4. Bake in a hot oven 200°C/400°F/gas mark 6 for 30 minutes until golden.

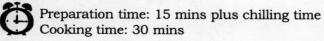
Preparation time: 15 mins plus chilling time
Cooking time: 30 mins

JANSEN'S QUICK TEMPTATION

This recipe is based on the famous potato dish.

Serves 4	Metric	Imperial	American
Can new potatoes	2 x 275 g	2 x 10 oz	2 x 10 oz
Garlic clove, crushed	1	1	1
Can anchovies	50 g	2 oz	2 oz
Butter, melted	75 g	3 oz	$^{1}/_{3}$ cup
Single (light) cream	150 ml	$^{1}/_{4}$ pt	$^{2}/_{3}$ cup
Breadcrumbs	50 g	2 oz	1 cup
Cheddar cheese, grated	50 g	2 oz	$^{1}/_{2}$ cup
To serve:			
Grated carrot and cucumber salad			

1. Drain and slice potatoes. Mix with the garlic and oil from the anchovies. Chop the fish and add.

2. Grease an ovenproof serving dish with some of the butter. Tip in potato mixture and level surface. Pour cream over.

3. Mix remaining butter with the breadcrumbs and cheese and sprinkle on top.

4. Bake at 200°C/400°C/gas mark 6 for about 35 minutes or until golden. Serve hot with a grated carrot and cucumber salad.

 Preparation time: 5 mins
Cooking time: 35 mins

SALMON IN FILO PASTRY

Serves 4–6	Metric	Imperial	American
Can red salmon	425 g	15 oz	15 oz
Filo pastry sheets	4-6	4-6	4-6
Butter, melted	50 g	2 oz	$1/4$ cup
Can creamed mushrooms	215 g	$7^1/2$ oz	$7^1/2$ oz
Dried basil or dill (dill weed)			
Passata (or sieved canned tomatoes)	60-90 ml	4-6 tbsp	4-6 tbsp
To garnish:			
Lemon wedges			
Sprigs of parsley (optional)			
To serve:			
New potatoes			
Green salad			

1. Drain salmon and carefully remove central backbone and any skin.

2. Lay a sheet of filo pastry on a board (keep remainder wrapped). Brush LIGHTLY with melted butter. Fold in half and brush lightly again. (NOTE: if sheets are small squares instead of larger rectangles, brush one with butter and top with a second sheet instead of folding - you will therefore need 8-12 sheets)

3. Place a spoonful of creamed mushrooms on centre of pastry. Top with $1/4$ or $1/6$ of the salmon (depending on how many you are making) and sprinkle with a good pinch of basil or dill.

4. Draw up over filling and pinch together to form a parcel pouch. Transfer to a lightly buttered baking sheet.

5. Repeat with remaining ingredients. Brush parcels with little more butter and bake in a hot oven 200°C/ 400°F/gas mark 6 for about 10-15 minutes until golden brown.

6. Meanwhile heat passata. When ready to serve, put parcels on warm serving plates. Put a spoonful of passata to one side of each parcel and garnish with lemon wedges and a sprig of parsley, if using. Serve with new potatoes and a crisp green salad.

 Preparation time: 10 mins
Cooking time: 10-15 mins

QUICK PARTY PAELLA

Serves 4	Metric	Imperial	American
Packet savoury mushroom or vegetable rice	*1*	*1*	*1*
Boiling water	*450 ml*	*³/₄ pt*	*2 cups*
Cooked chicken, diced	*100 g*	*4 oz*	*1 cup*
Can mussels, drained	*250 g*	*9 oz*	*9 oz*
Frozen prawns (shrimp)	*100 g*	*4 oz*	*1 cup*
To serve:			
Crusty bread			
Salad			

1. Put rice in a pan with the boiling water. Stir, cover and simmer for 12 minutes.

2. Add remaining ingredients, stir, cover and simmer gently for a further 8 minutes until all the liquid has been absorbed and the rice is tender. Serve with crusty bread and salad.

 Preparation time: 4 mins
Cooking time: 20 mins

SALMON FLAN

Freeze the rest of the canned pimiento caps and anchovies for use at a later date.

Serves 4	Metric	Imperial	American
Shortcrust pastry (basic pie crust)	*175 g*	*6 oz*	*¹/₃ lb*
Packet white sauce mix	*1*	*1*	*1*
Milk or water (according to packet)	*300 ml*	*¹/₂ pt*	*1¹/₄ cups*
Can salmon	*185 g*	*6 ¹/₂ oz*	*6 ¹/₂ oz*
Tomato purée (paste)	*15 ml*	*1 tbsp*	*1 tbsp*
Canned pimiento cap, chopped	*1*	*1*	*1*
Canned anchovy fillets	*5*	*5*	*5*
Stuffed olives, halved	*3*	*3*	*3*
To serve:			
Crusty bread			
Salad			

1. Roll out pastry and use to line an 18 cm/7 in flan dish (pie pan). Prick base with a fork then line with crumpled foil and bake at 200°C/400°F/gas mark 6 for 10 minutes. Remove foil and bake for a further 5 minutes until golden brown.

2. Meanwhile, make up white sauce according to packet directions. Flake fish, discarding bones and skin and add to sauce with tomato purée and chopped pimiento.

3. If serving hot, reheat.

4.   Turn into pastry case (shell), decorate with anchovies and olives and serve hot. Alternatively, leave until cold before serving with crusty bread and salad.

 Preparation time: 5 mins
Cooking time: 15 mins plus cooling time if wished

SEASIDE CRUMBLE

Serves 4	Metric	Imperial	American
Topping:			
Plain (all-purpose) flour	*75 g*	*3 oz*	*³/₄ cup*
Soft butter or margarine	*40 g*	*1¹/₂ oz*	*3 tbsp*
Cheddar cheese, grated	*50 g*	*2 oz*	*¹/₂ cup*
Filling:			
Frozen white fish fillets	*450 g*	*1 lb*	*1 lb*
Can condensed celery soup	*295 g*	*10¹/₂ oz*	*10¹/₂ oz*
Frozen mixed vegetables	*100 g*	*4 oz*	*1 cup*
Chopped parsley	*15 ml*	*1 tbsp*	*1 tbsp*

1.   Put flour in a bowl, work in the butter or margarine with a fork until crumbly. Stir in the cheese.

2.   Cut fish into small dice, discarding any skin and any bones.

3.   Place in an ovenproof serving dish and mix in the soup, vegetables and parsley.

4.   Spoon crumble over and bake in a hot oven 200°C/ 400°F/gas mark 6 for about 30 minutes until golden brown and cooked through.

 Preparation time: 5 mins
Cooking time: 30 mins

SAUCY COD PUFFS

Serves 4	Metric	Imperial	American
Frozen puff pastry (paste), just thawed	350 g	12 oz	12 oz
Tomatoes, chopped (optional)	2	2	2
Frozen cod steaks in parsley sauce	4	4	4
Beaten egg, to glaze			
To serve:			
Creamed potatoes			
Green beans			

1. Cut pastry into quarters. Roll out and trim each to about 18 cm/7 in square.

2. If using tomatoes, divide among the four pastry pieces.

3. Carefully remove fish and sauce from bag and place on top of tomato.

4. Brush edges of pastry with beaten egg and fold over fish to form parcels. Press edges well together to seal.

5. Transfer parcels sealed sides down to a dampened baking sheet. Brush with beaten egg. Make 'leaves' out of any pastry trimmings, place on parcels and brush with a little more egg.

6. Bake at 220°C/425°F/gas mark 7 for 15-20 minutes until puffy, golden and cooked through. Serve hot with creamed potatoes and green beans.

Preparation time: 10 mins
Cooking time: 15-20 mins

FISHERMAN'S PIZZA

Serves 2–4	Metric	Imperial	American
Pizza base (ready made)	23 cm	9 in	9 in
Tomato purée (paste)	45 ml	3 tbsp	3 tbsp
Packet cheese sauce mix	1	1	1
Milk or water (according to packet but a little less than recommended)	250 ml	8 fl oz	1 cup
Can sild in oil (or small sardines), drained	120 g	4½ oz	4½ oz
Cheddar cheese, grated	50 g	2 oz	½ cup
To garnish:			
Chopped parsley			
To serve:			
Jacket potatoes			
Tomato and onion salad			

1. Put pizza base on a baking sheet.

2. Spread with tomato purée to within 1 cm/½ in of edge.

3. Make up cheese sauce using less than the recommended amount of milk and water (to give a thicker consistency).

4. Spread over tomato purée. Arrange drained sild in a starburst pattern on top and sprinkle with grated cheese.

5. Bake in a hot oven 220°C/425°F/gas mark 7 for about 20 minutes or until golden and bubbling. Serve hot with jacket potatoes and tomato and onion salad.

Preparation time: 5 mins
Cooking time: 20 mins

FISH MOUSSE

Serves 6–8	Metric	Imperial	American
Can tuna or salmon	425 g	15 oz	15 oz
Sachet powdered gelatine	1	1	1
Water	30 ml	2 tbsp	2 tbsp
Mayonnaise	45 ml	3 tbsp	3 tbsp
Tomato purée (paste)	15 ml	1 tbsp	1 tbsp
Anchovy essence (extract) (optional)	10 ml	2 tsp	2 tsp
Lemon juice	30 ml	2 tbsp	2 tbsp
Salt and pepper			
Double (heavy) or whipping cream	300 ml	1/2 pt	1 1/4 cups
To serve:			
Mixed salads			

1. Drain fish and mash well, discarding any skin and bones.

2. Dissolve gelatine in the water according to packet directions.

3. Add mayonnaise, tomato purée, anchovy essence, if using, lemon juice and a little salt and pepper and beat well. Beat in dissolved gelatine.

4. Whip cream until softly peaking and fold into fish mixture with a metal spoon. Turn into an oiled fish or jelly (jello) mould (mold) or an attractive serving dish. Chill until set.

5. Just before serving turn out, if necessary, onto a serving plate and serve with mixed salads.

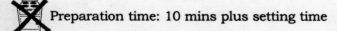 Preparation time: 10 mins plus setting time

PEPPERED TROUT

Serves 4	Metric	Imperial	American
Frozen rainbow trout, just thawed	*4*	*4*	*4*
Oil	*15 ml*	*1 tbsp*	*1 tbsp*
Butter or margarine	*15 ml*	*1 tbsp*	*1 tbsp*
Sauce:			
Soft cheese with black pepper	*80 g*	*3¼ oz*	*3¼ oz*
Milk	*45 ml*	*3 tbsp*	*3 tbsp*
To garnish:			
Chopped parsley			
To serve:			
Sautéed potatoes			
Broccoli			

1. Rinse fish, dry on kitchen paper and cut off heads, if preferred.

2. Heat oil and butter or margarine in a large frying pan (skillet) and fry (sauté) fish for 5 minutes on each side until cooked through. Transfer to a warmed serving plate and keep warm.

3. Strain cooking juices into a saucepan (to avoid any bits of skin in sauce). Add cheese and 30 ml/2 tbsp milk. Heat through gently, stirring until cheese melts. Add a little more milk until sauce is pouring consistency.

4. Pour over fish, sprinkle with chopped parsley and serve with sautéed potatoes and broccoli.

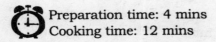 Preparation time: 4 mins
Cooking time: 12 mins

CRAB THERMIDOR

Serves 4	Metric	Imperial	American
Packet white sauce mix	1	1	1
Milk or water (according to packet, but a little less than recommended)	250 ml	8 fl oz	1 cup
Brandy	15 ml	1 tbsp	1 tbsp
Dijon mustard	5 ml	1 tsp	1 tsp
Dried mixed herbs	2.5 ml	¹/₂ tsp	¹/₂ tsp
Cans white crabmeat	2 x 175 g	2 x 6 oz	2 x 6 oz
Breadcrumbs	50 g	2 oz	1 cup
Butter or margarine, melted	25 g	1 oz	2 tbsp
Cheddar cheese, grated	50 g	2 oz	¹/₂ cup
To garnish:			
Parsley			
To serve:			
New potatoes			
Crisp green salad			

1. Make up sauce using slightly less than the recommended amount of liquid. Stir in the brandy, mustard and herbs.

2. Spoon a layer of half the sauce into the base of 4 individual gratin or other shallow fireproof dishes.

3. Top with drained crabmeat then cover with the rest of the sauce.

4. Mix breadcrumbs with melted butter and the grated cheese. Sprinkle over. Place under a moderate grill (broiler) until golden brown and heated through, about 5-8 minutes. Serve with new potatoes and a crisp green salad.

 Preparation time: 5 mins
Cooking time: 8-10 mins

QUICK FISH POT

Serves 4	Metric	Imperial	American
Frozen white fish fillet	*350 g*	*12 oz*	*12 oz*
Can chopped tomatoes	*400 g*	*14 oz*	*14 oz*
Vegetable or fish stock	*300 ml*	*¹/₂ pt*	*1¹/₄ cups*
Anchovy essence (extract)	*5 ml*	*1 tsp*	*1 tsp*
Can new potatoes, drained			
* and quartered*	*275 g*	*10 oz*	*10 oz*
Can sliced carrots, drained	*275 g*	*10 oz*	*10 oz*
Can garden peas, drained	*275 g*	*10 oz*	*10 oz*
Salt and pepper			
To garnish:			
Chopped parsley			
To serve:			
Crusty bread			

1. Cut fish into small chunks, discarding skin and any bones.

2. Place tomatoes and stock in a large saucepan. Add remaining ingredients, adding fish last.

3. Bring to the boil, reduce heat, cover and simmer for 5 minutes until fish is tender. Stir gently and season to taste. Ladle into large, warm soup bowls, garnish with parsley and serve with lots of crusty bread.

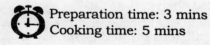 Preparation time: 3 mins
Cooking time: 5 mins

SMOKED HADDOCK FLORENTINE

Use white fish if you prefer.

Serves 4	Metric	Imperial	American
Frozen chopped spinach	450 g	1 lb	2 cups
Boil in the bag smoked haddock	2 x 175 g	2 x 6 oz	2 x 6 oz
Packet cheese sauce mix	1	1	1
Milk or water (according to packet)	300 ml	1/2 pt	1 1/4 cups
A little grated Cheddar cheese (optional)			
To serve:			
Poached eggs			
Triangles of crisp toast			
Canned or stewed, fresh tomatoes			

1. Cook spinach according to packet directions. Drain and spread in base of a 1.2 L/2 pt/5 cup flameproof dish.

2. Cook fish according to packet directions. Lay on top of spinach.

3. Make up sauce according to packet directions. Spoon over. Cover with grated cheese, if using.

4. Place under a hot grill (broiler) until golden and bubbling. Serve with poached eggs, if liked, triangles of crisp toast and canned or stewed fresh tomatoes.

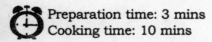 Preparation time: 3 mins
Cooking time: 10 mins

SPAGHETTI WITH CLAMS

Serves 4	Metric	Imperial	American
Spaghetti	350 g	12 oz	3/4 lb
Salt			
Sauce:			
Onion, chopped	1	1	1
Garlic clove, crushed	1	1	1
Olive oil	15 ml	1 tbsp	1 tbsp
Passata (sieved tomatoes)	300 ml	1/2 pt	1 1/4 cups
Can baby clams	300 g	11 oz	11 oz
Salt and black pepper			
To garnish:			
Chopped parsley			
To serve:			
Green salad			

1. Cook spaghetti in plenty of boiling, salted water for 10 minutes or until just tender, drain.

2. Meanwhile, fry (sauté) onion and garlic in the oil for 3 minutes, stirring, until soft but not brown. Add passata, drained clams and a little salt and pepper and simmer for 5 minutes.

3. Add to spaghetti and toss well. Garnish with chopped parsley and serve with a green salad.

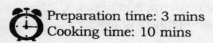 Preparation time: 3 mins
Cooking time: 10 mins

SMOKY JACKETS

Serves 4	Metric	Imperial	American
Potatoes, large	4	4	4
Butter or margarine	25 g	1 oz	2 tbsp
Low fat soft cheese	225g	8 oz	1 cup
Can smoked mussels	100 g	4 oz	4 oz
Chopped (snipped) chives or parsley	15 ml	1 tbsp	1 tbsp
Lemon juice			
Salt and pepper			
To serve:			
Mixed salad			

1. Scrub potatoes. Make a cut lengthwise round centre of each potato, ready to cut in halves when cooked.

2. Boil in water for about 20 minutes or until tender. (Or bake in a moderate oven for about 1 hour or microwave or pressure cook according to appliance instructions).

3. Cut potatoes into halves and scoop out most of the flesh into a bowl, leaving a 'shell' of skin and potato.

4. Mash flesh with butter or margarine and cheese.

5. Drain mussels and roughly chop, or leave whole as preferred. Mix with the potato, add herbs, a little lemon juice and salt and pepper to taste.

6. Pile back into shells and place under a moderate grill (broiler) for about 5 minutes or until golden and hot through. Serve with a mixed salad.

 Preparation time: 8 mins
Cooking time: about 30 mins

MADAME BOVARY'S OMELETTE

Serves 4	Metric	Imperial	American
Small onion, finely chopped	*1*	*1*	*1*
Butter	*125 g*	*5 oz*	*good ½ cup*
Cans soft cod roes	*2 x 100 g*	*2 x 4 oz*	*2 x 4 oz*
Can tuna	*100 g*	*4 oz*	*4 oz*
Eggs, beaten	*8*	*8*	*8*
Salt and pepper			
Chopped parsley	*15 g*	*1 tbsp*	*1 tbsp*
Dried mixed herbs	*5 ml*	*1 tsp*	*1 tsp*
Lemon juice			
To serve:			
French bread			

1. Fry (sauté) onion in 50 g/2 oz/¼ cup of the butter until soft, but not brown, about 3 minutes.

2. Drain roes and tuna and mix with onion. Stir into beaten eggs and season.

3. Melt 10 g/¼ oz/½ tbsp remaining butter in an omelette pan, add a quarter of the mixture. Lift and stir egg gently in pan until just set and golden underneath. Fold in three and slide onto a warmed serving plate. Keep warm while you make three more omelettes.

4. Melt remaining butter and stir in the parsley, mixed herbs and a little lemon juice to taste. Pour a little around each omelette and serve with French bread.

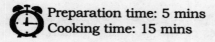 Preparation time: 5 mins
Cooking time: 15 mins

CRAB AND CHEESE TART

Serves 4	Metric	Imperial	American
Butter, melted	50 g	2 oz	1/4 cup
Filo pastry sheets	8	8	8
Can crab meat	175 g	6 oz	6 oz
Port Salut or St Paulin cheese	175 g	6 oz	1/3 lb
Eggs	3	3	3
Crème fraîche (or single (light) cream)	300 ml	1/2 pt	1 1/4 cups
Salt and pepper			
Dried thyme	2.5 ml	1/2 tsp	1/2 tsp
To serve:			
Green salad			

1. Lightly butter a 20 cm/8 in flan dish (pie pan).

2. Layer sheets of pastry in dish, brushing with butter between layers, allowing edges of pastry to hang over sides of dish.

3. Drain crab and spread on pastry base.

4. Cut orange rind off cheese thinly and discard. Slice cheese and lay over crab.

5. Beat eggs with crème fraîche, a little salt and pepper and the thyme. Pour over filling then gently fold pastry flaps over top. Brush top lightly with butter.

6. Bake in a moderate oven 180°C/350°F/gas mark 4 for about 30-35 minutes or until set and golden. Serve warm with a green salad.

 Preparation time: 5 mins
Cooking time: 35 mins

MEAT AND POULTRY

Even today, for many people if a main meal doesn't contain meat of some sort, it isn't a proper meal! I don't subscribe to that myself, but can thoroughly recommend all the following recipes as filling, tasty and meaty enough for even the hungriest appetite. Sometimes all you need is a little imagination stirred into your favourite recipes: such as adding a spoonful of herbs to your toad in the hole batter and serving it with a packet of onion sauce.

You can do interesting things with leftovers from your roasts, too. Dice cooked chicken and mix it with enough mayonnaise to coat, flavoured with a little curry powder and mango chutney. Try your Curried Chicken Mayonnaise with a packet of savoury rice, cooked and cooled – delicious.

BEEF IN WINE

Serves 4–6	Metric	Imperial	American
Onion, finely chopped	1	1	1
Oil	15 ml	1 tbsp	1 tbsp
Cans stewed steak without gravy	2 x 440 g	2 x 15¹/₂ oz	2 x 15¹/₂ oz
Red wine	300 ml	¹/₂ pt	1¹/₄ cups
Can button mushrooms	300 g	11 oz	11 oz
Can sliced carrots	275 g	10 oz	10 oz
Dried mixed herbs	2.5 ml	¹/₂ tsp	¹/₂ tsp
Caster (superfine) sugar	pinch	pinch	pinch
Cornflour (cornstarch)	20 ml	4 tsp	4 tsp
Salt and pepper			
To serve:			
Creamed potatoes			
Broccoli			

1. Fry (sauté) onion in the oil for 3 minutes until soft but not brown.

2. Add steak and wine and heat through, stirring to break up meat.

3. Drain mushrooms and carrots, reserving 30 ml/2 tbsp of the mushroom liquid.

4. Add vegetables, herbs and sugar to pan and continue to heat through gently until bubbling.

5. Blend cornflour with the reserved mushroom liquid. Stir gently into pan and cook until thickened. Taste and season if necessary. Serve with creamed potatoes and broccoli.

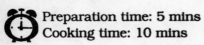 Preparation time: 5 mins
Cooking time: 10 mins

INTERNATIONAL BEEF POT

Serves 4–6	Metric	Imperial	American
Cans stewed steak with or without gravy	2 x 440 g	2 x 15½ oz	2 x 15½ oz
Can water chestnuts	225 g	8 oz	8 oz
Can condensed mushroom soup	295 g	10½ oz	10½ oz
Potatoes, thinly sliced	450 g	1 lb	1 lb
To garnish:			
Parsley			
To serve:			
A green vegetable			

1.   Empty meat into a large shallow ovenproof dish and break up with a wooden spoon.

2.   Drain and slice water chestnuts and scatter over.

3.   Spoon over half the can of soup.

4.   Arrange sliced potatoes neatly in a single layer over top.

5.   Thin remaining soup slightly with water and spoon over.

6.   Bake in a hot oven 200°C/400°F/gas mark 6 for about 45 minutes until potatoes are cooked and top is golden brown. Garnish with parsley and serve with a green vegetable.

Preparation time: 5 mins
Cooking time: 45 mins

BEEF IN BEER

Serves 4–6	Metric	Imperial	American
Cans stewed steak in gravy	2 x 440 g	2 x 15¹/₂ oz	2 x 15¹/₂ oz
Beer	60 ml	4 tbsp	4 tbsp
Brandy	15 ml	1 tbsp	1 tbsp
Instant mashed potato	30 ml	2 tbsp	2 tbsp
French bread slices	6-8	6-8	6-8
Butter	25 g	1 oz	2 tbsp
Grainy mustard	15 ml	1 tbsp	1 tbsp
To serve:			
Boiled potatoes			
Green beans			

1. Empty cans of meat into a saucepan with the beer and brandy. Stir well. Heat through until bubbling.

2. Sprinkle instant mashed potato over and stir in to thicken. Turn into a flameproof casserole (Dutch oven).

3. Meanwhile toast slices of French bread on one side. Mash butter and mustard together and spread on untoasted sides.

4. Arrange around top of carbonnade. Place under a hot grill (broiler) until toasted and bubbling. Serve hot with boiled potatoes and green beans.

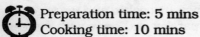 Preparation time: 5 mins
Cooking time: 10 mins

Note:

All the following mince (ground) beef recipes can be made with 225 g/8 oz/2 cups frozen meat instead of a can. Dry-fry the meat with a chopped onion then add 300 ml/½ pt/1¼ cups beef stock and simmer for 10 minutes. Thicken with 15 ml/1 tbsp cornflour (cornstarch) blended with a little water and add a few drops of gravy browning and seasoning to taste. Then continue as described in recipes.

PASTA GRILL

Serves 4	Metric	Imperial	American
Pasta shapes	225 g	8 oz	2 cups
Can minced (ground) steak			
with onions	425 g	15 oz	15 oz
Dried mixed herbs	5 ml	1 tsp	1 tsp
Cheddar cheese, grated	50 g	2 oz	½ cup
Tomatoes, sliced (optional)	2-3	2-3	2-3
To serve:			
Salad			

1. Cook pasta according to packet directions. Drain, rinse with hot water and drain again.

2. Return to saucepan and add contents of can of mince and season with herbs.

3. Heat through, stirring gently until piping hot.

4. Turn into a flameproof dish, sprinkle cheese over and arrange tomato slices around edge, if using.

5. Brown under a hot grill (broiler) for about 3 minutes then serve hot with salad.

 Preparation time: 2 mins
Cooking time: about 15 mins

QUICK MEXICAN MEAL

For less fire, use half the amount of chilli powder.

Serves 4	Metric	Imperial	American
Can minced (ground) steak with onions	425 g	15 oz	15 oz
Tomato purée (paste)	15 ml	1 tbsp	1 tbsp
Chilli powder	2.5 ml	1/2 tsp	1/2 tsp
Garlic clove, crushed	1	1	1
Can red kidney beans, drained	425 g	15 oz	15 oz
Taco shells	12	12	12
To serve:			
Shredded lettuce			
Chopped tomato			
Soured (dairy sour) cream			
Grated Cheddar cheese			

1. Put mince in a pan with the tomato purée, chilli powder, garlic and beans. Heat through, stirring until bubbling.

2. Warm taco shells in a hot oven or the microwave according to packet directions. Spoon chilli mixture into shells and serve with shredded lettuce, chopped tomato, and soured cream and cheese to spoon on top of the meat.

 Preparation time: 5 mins
Cooking time: 5 mins

TOWN HOUSE PIE

Serves 4	Metric	Imperial	American
Can minced (ground) steak with onion	*425 g*	*15 oz*	*15 oz*
Can baked beans in tomato sauce	*225 g*	*8 oz*	*8 oz*
Worcestershire sauce	*10 ml*	*2 tsp*	*2 tsp*
Dried thyme	*2.5 ml*	*1/2 tsp*	*1/2 tsp*
Instant mashed potato, servings	*4*	*4*	*4*
Cheddar cheese, grated	*50 g*	*2 oz*	*1/2 cup*
To serve:			
Crusty bread			
A green vegetable			

1. Put meat, beans, Worcestershire sauce and thyme in a saucepan and heat through until piping hot, stirring occasionally. Turn into a flameproof dish (or put in dish and heat in microwave).

2. Meanwhile make up potato according to packet directions. Pile on top of meat mixture and sprinkle with cheese.

3. Place under a hot grill (broiler) until golden and bubbling. Serve with crusty bread and a green vegetable.

 Preparation time: 5 mins
Cooking time: about 5 mins

SAVOURY STRUDEL

Serves 4	Metric	Imperial	American
Filo pastry sheets	*4*	*4*	*4*
Butter, melted	*25 g*	*1 oz*	*2 tbsp*
Can minced (ground) steak			
with onion	*425 g*	*15 oz*	*15 oz*
Grated nutmeg	*pinch*	*pinch*	*pinch*
Passata (sieved tomatoes)	*90 ml*	*6 tbsp*	*6 tbsp*
To serve:			
Sweetcorn (corn)			

1. Brush a sheet of filo pastry lightly with butter, lay another sheet on top. Continue layering in this way.

2. Gently spread meat mixture over pastry to within 1 cm/½ in of the edge all round.

3. Sprinkle with a little grated nutmeg.

4. Fold in short sides of pastry then roll up from a long end.

5. Carefully transfer strudel to a lightly buttered baking sheet and shape it into a curve. Brush with a little more butter.

6. Bake in a hot oven 200°C/400°F/gas mark 6 for about 20 minutes or until crisp and golden brown. Carefully transfer to a warm serving platter. Heat passata and spoon around. Serve hot with sweetcorn.

 Preparation time: 5 mins
Cooking time: about 20 mins

POTATO MOUSSAKA

Serves 4	Metric	Imperial	American
Potatoes, scrubbed and sliced (not peeled) (or a large can)	450 g	1 lb	1 lb
Salt			
Can minced (ground) steak with onion	425 g	15 oz	15 oz
Garlic clove, crushed	1	1	1
Tomato purée (paste)	15 ml	1 tbsp	1 tbsp
Cinnamon	5 ml	1 tsp	1 tsp
Plain yoghurt or single (light) cream	150 ml	¼ pt	⅔ cup
Egg	1	1	1
Salt and pepper			
Cheddar cheese, grated	50 g	2 oz	½ cup
To serve:			
Salad			

1. Boil potatoes in salted water for about 5 minutes until tender. Drain. Or drain and slice canned potatoes.

2. Mix mince with garlic, tomato purée and cinnamon. Layer potatoes and meat mixture in an ovenproof serving dish, finishing with a layer of potatoes.

3. Beat yoghurt or cream with the egg and a little salt and pepper. Stir in the cheese. Pour over potatoes.

4. Bake in a moderately hot oven 190°C/375°F/gas mark 5 for about 35 minutes until bubbling, golden and top has set. Or cook in a microwave and brown under grill (broiler).

5. Serve with salad.

Preparation time: 5 mins
Cooking time: about 35 mins

PAN HASH

Serves 4	Metric	Imperial	American
Onions, chopped	2	2	2
Oil	30 ml	2 tbsp	2 tbsp
Cooked potatoes, diced	450 g	1 lb	2 cups
Can corned beef, diced	350 g	12 oz	12 oz
Can baked beans in tomato sauce	425 g	15 oz	15 oz
Brown table sauce	15 ml	1 tbsp	1 tbsp
Salt and pepper			
To serve:			
Crusty bread			
Salad			

1. Fry (sauté) onion in the oil for 3 minutes until soft but not brown.

2. Mix remaining ingredients together. Add to pan and fry, for 5 minutes turning mixture over occasionally.

3. Press down with a fish slice and continue frying for a further 5 minutes without disturbing until crisp and brown underneath. Serve straight from the pan with crusty bread and salad.

 Preparation time: 5 mins
Cooking time: about 13 mins

CORNED-ISH PASTIES

Serves 4	Metric	Imperial	American
Shortcrust pastry (basic pie crust)	350 g	12 oz	³/₄ lb
Filling:			
Can corned beef, diced small	185 g	6¹/₂ oz	6¹/₂ oz
Can mixed vegetables, drained	275 g	10 oz	10 oz
Pepper			
Egg, beaten, to glaze	1	1	1
To serve:			
Coleslaw			
Green salad			

1. Cut pastry into quarters, roll out each one to an 18-20 cm/7-8 in circle, using a plate or saucepan lid as a guide.

2. Divide meat and vegetables between centres of four pastry circles. Season with pepper. Brush edges with beaten egg and draw up over filling, pressing edges well together to seal. Crimp between finger and thumb.

3. Transfer to a baking sheet. Brush with beaten egg to glaze and bake in a hot oven 200°C/400°F/gas mark 6 for about 15-20 minutes until golden brown. Serve hot or cold with coleslaw and green salad.

 Preparation time: 10 mins
Cooking time 15-20 mins

MIDWEEK BEEF WELLINGTON

Serves 4–6	Metric	Imperial	American
Large onion, chopped	1	1	1
Oil	15 ml	1 tbsp	1 tbsp
Can sliced mushrooms, drained	300 g	11 oz	11 oz
Sweet pickle	15 ml	1 tbsp	1 tbsp
Frozen puff pastry, thawed	450 g	1 lb	1 lb
Can corned beef	350 g	12 oz	12 oz
Egg, beaten, to glaze			
To serve:			
Sweetcorn (corn)			
Passata (or sieved canned tomatoes)			

1. Fry onion in the oil for 3 minutes until soft, not brown. Stir in the mushrooms and sweet pickle and leave to cool.

2. Roll out pastry to a rectangle about 25 cm x 18 cm/ 10 in x 7 in.

3. Spoon onion mixture into centre of pastry, put corned beef on top.

4. Brush edges of pastry with beaten egg, fold over filling and press well together to seal.

5. Place sealed sides down on a dampened baking sheet.

6. Make a criss-cross pattern over pastry with a sharp knife and brush all over with beaten egg.

7. Bake in a hot oven 220°C/425°F/gas mark 7 for 30 minutes, covering lightly with foil if over browning. Serve hot with sweetcorn and hot passata as a sauce.

 Preparation time: 10 mins
Cooking time: 33 mins

CORNED BEEF STUFFED PANCAKES

Serves 4	Metric	Imperial	American
Can corned beef	350 g	12 oz	12 oz
Tomato ketchup (catsup)	30 ml	2 tbsp	2 tbsp
Sweet pickle	15 ml	1 tbsp	1 tbsp
Packet pancake batter mix	1	1	1
Egg (if necessary)	1	1	1
Milk or water (according to packets)	600 ml	1 pt	2½ cups
Oil			
Packet cheese sauce mix	1	1	1
To serve:			
Salad			

1. Chop corned beef and mix with tomato ketchup and pickle. Heat through gently until piping hot.

2. Meanwhile make up pancake batter with egg, if necessary, and 300 ml/½ pt/1¼ cups of liquid.

3. Heat a little oil in a frying pan (skillet), pour off excess. Add about 30 ml/2 tbsp of the batter, swirl round to coat base of pan. Fry (sauté) until underside is golden. Turn over and brown other side. Slide out of pan and keep warm while cooking remaining pancakes in same way.

4. Spread a little of the filling on each pancake, roll up and keep hot while making sauce according to packet directions with the remaining liquid. Pour over centre of pancakes and serve hot with salad.

Preparation time: 10 mins
Cooking time: about 30 mins

MEDITERRANEAN LAMB CHOPS

If you want to go out, pop these in a moderate oven for an hour or longer – instead of cooking them on top of the stove.

Serves 4	Metric	Imperial	American
Frozen lamb chops, thawed	*4*	*4*	*4*
Oil	*15 ml*	*1 tbsp*	*1 tbsp*
Onion, chopped	*1*	*1*	*1*
Salt and pepper			
Can condensed tomato soup	*295 g*	*10½ oz*	*10½ oz*
Dried basil	*5 ml*	*1 tsp*	*1 tsp*
To garnish:			
Black olives			
To serve:			
Buttered noodles			

1. Fry (sauté) chops in the oil on each side to brown.

2. Remove from pan and fry onion for 3 minutes until soft and turning golden. Drain off fat from pan.

3. Return chops, sprinkle with salt and pepper and spoon soup over. Add herbs.

4. Bring to the boil, reduce heat, cover and simmer very gently for 45 minutes or until chops are really tender. Stir gently occasionally and add a little water if necessary. Garnish with black olives and serve with buttered noodles.

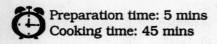 Preparation time: 5 mins
Cooking time: 45 mins

GREEK-STYLE LAMB LUNCH

Serves 4	Metric	Imperial	American
Frozen minced (ground) lambsteaks	4	4	4
Plain yoghurt	150 ml	1/4 pt	2/3 cup
Garlic clove, crushed	1	1	1
Dried mint	5 ml	1 tsp	1 tsp
Salt and pepper			
Pitta breads	4	4	4
To garnish:			
Shredded lettuce			
Grated cucumber			
Chopped tomato			

1. Grill (broil), fry (sauté) or microwave lambsteaks according to packet instructions.

2. Meanwhile mix yoghurt with the garlic, mint and a little salt and pepper.

3. Grill (broil) or microwave pittas to warm. Make a slit along one long edge of each and open up to form a pocket.

4. Put a lambsteak in each pocket. Spoon in the yoghurt mixture and garnish each with shredded lettuce, grated cucumber and chopped tomato.

 Preparation time: 5 mins
Cooking time: about 10 mins

LAMBS' TONGUES IN CAPER SAUCE

Serves 4	Metric	Imperial	American
Can lambs' tongues	350 g	12 oz	12 oz
Packet white sauce mix	1	1	1
Milk or water (according to packet)	300 ml	¹/₂ pt	1¹/₄ cups
Capers, chopped	15 ml	1 tbsp	1 tbsp
Instant mashed potato servings	4	4	4
To garnish:			
Chopped parsley	15 ml	1 tbsp	1 tbsp
To serve:			
Peas			

1. Cut lambs' tongues into neat slices.

2. Make up white sauce according to packet directions. Stir in the capers.

3. Add meat to sauce and heat through until piping hot – about 5 minutes.

4. Meanwhile, make up potato and spoon into "nests" in 4 flameproof dishes. Brown under a hot grill (broiler). Spoon meat and sauce into centre of nests, garnish with chopped parsley and serve withpeas.

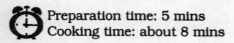
Preparation time: 5 mins
Cooking time: about 8 mins

PAN CASSEROLED CHICKEN

This dish is also excellent cooked in a moderate oven for about 1 hour.

Serves 4	Metric	Imperial	American
Frozen chicken portions, *thawed*	*4*	*4*	*4*
Plain (all-purpose) flour	*30 ml*	*2 tbsp*	*2 tbsp*
Salt and pepper			
Butter	*40 g*	*1½ oz*	*3 tbsp*
Curry powder or paste	*5 ml*	*1 tsp*	*1 tsp*
Can condensed cream of *mushroom soup*	*295 g*	*10½ oz*	*10½ oz*
To serve:			
Plain boiled rice			
Sprouts			

1.   Wipe chicken with kitchen paper. Mix flour with a little salt and pepper and use to coat chicken.

2.   Melt butter in a flameproof casserole (Dutch oven) and fry (sauté) chicken on all sides to brown.

3.   Take chicken out of casserole. Drain off all but 15 ml/ 1 tbsp of the fat. Stir in curry powder or paste and fry for 1 minute. Blend in the soup.

4.   Return chicken to the pan, bring to the boil, reduce heat to as low as possible, cover and simmer for 45 minutes until chicken is tender. Stir occasionally and add a little water if necessary to prevent sticking. Serve with boiled rice and sprouts.

 Preparation time: 5 mins
Cooking time: 50 mins

CHUNKY CHICKEN PARCELS WITH CRANBERRY

Serves 4	Metric	Imperial	American
Filo pastry sheets	*4*	*4*	*4*
Melted butter	*50 g*	*2 oz*	*¼ cup*
Can chunky chicken	*425 g*	*15 oz*	*15 oz*
Dried mixed herbs	*5 ml*	*1 tsp*	*1 tsp*
Sauce:			
Cranberry sauce	*60 ml*	*4 tbsp*	*4 tbsp*
Port	*15 ml*	*1 tbsp*	*1 tbsp*
To garnish:			
Parsley			
To serve:			
New potatoes			
Asparagus spears			

1. Lay a filo pastry sheet on work surface. Brush lightly with melted butter and fold in half. Brush with butter again.

2. Put a quarter of the chicken in centre of pastry, sprinkle with 1.5 ml/¼ tsp herbs.

3. Draw pastry up over filling to form a pouch. Transfer to a buttered baking sheet and brush with a little melted butter. Repeat with remaining ingredients.

4. Bake in a hot oven 200°C/400°F/gas mark 6 for 10-15 minutes until golden brown.

5. Meanwhile heat cranberry sauce and port together in a saucepan. Transfer chicken parcels to warm serving plates. Spoon a little of the sauce around each and garnish with parsley before serving with new potatoes and asparagus spears.

 Preparation time: 8 mins
Cooking time: 10-15 mins

ROSY CHICKEN SALAD

Serves 4–6	Metric	Imperial	American
Whole ready cooked chicken	1.5 kg	3 lb	3 lb
Sauce:			
Mayonnaise	150 ml	¼ pt	⅔ cup
Milk	15 ml	1 tbsp	1 tbsp
Tomato purée (paste)	15 ml	1 tbsp	1 tbsp
Piece cucumber, finely diced	5 cm	2 in	2 in
Blanched whole almonds	50 g	2 oz	½ cup
Butter or margarine	15 g	½ oz	1 tbsp
Chilli powder	1.5 ml	¼ tsp	¼ tsp
Mixed (apple pie) spice	1.5 ml	¼ tsp	¼ tsp
Lettuce			
To serve:			
Potatoes boiled in their skins			
Salad			

1. Joint chicken into six pieces and carve the breast. Alternatively cut all meat off bones, discard skin, leave meat in chunky pieces.

2. Blend mayonnaise, milk, tomato purée and cucumber together.

3. Fry (sauté) almonds in the butter until golden brown. Sprinkle with spices and toss well. Drain on kitchen paper.

4. Arrange chicken attractively on a bed of lettuce. Spoon mayonnaise mixture over and scatter with almonds. Serve with potatoes boiled in their skins and salad.

 Preparation time: 10 mins
Cooking time: about 3 mins (for almonds)

MAYBE CHICKEN CHOW MEIN

Serves 4	Metric	Imperial	American
Quick-cook Chinese egg noodles	*225 g*	*8 oz*	*2 cups*
Cooked chicken, cut in strips	*225 g*	*8 oz*	*¹/₂ lb*
Can stir-fry mixed vegetables, drained	*425 g*	*15 oz*	*15 oz*
Garlic clove, crushed	*1*	*1*	*1*
Soy sauce	*30 ml*	*2 tbsp*	*2 tbsp*
Sherry	*30 ml*	*2 tbsp*	*2 tbsp*
Ground ginger	*5 ml*	*1 tsp*	*1 tsp*
Brown sugar	*15 ml*	*1 tbsp*	*1 tbsp*
To garnish:			
Cashew nuts (optional)			

1.   Cook noodles according to packet directions. Drain.

2.   Put all remaining ingredients in a large pan or wok and heat through, stirring occasionally until piping hot.

3.   Stir in noodles, reheat and serve garnished with cashew nuts if liked.

 Preparation time: 10 mins
Cooking time: 10 mins

MOCK PEKING DUCK

You will find flour tortillas in the supermarket near the pitta breads and bagels. Alternatively use pittas and fill rather than roll up.

Serves 4	Metric	Imperial	American
Spring onions (scallions), bunch	1	1	1
Cucumber	¼	¼	¼
Turkey stir-fry pieces	450 g	1 lb	1 lb
Flour tortillas	12	12	12
Oil	15 ml	1 tbsp	1 tbsp
Marinade:			
Soy sauce	30 ml	2 tbsp	2 tbsp
Ground ginger	2.5 ml	½ tsp	½ tsp
Garlic clove, crushed	1	1	1
Red wine vinegar	15 ml	1 tbsp	1 tbsp
Pepper			
Plum Sauce:			
Plum jam (conserve)	60 ml	4 tbsp	4 tbsp
Soy sauce	30 ml	2 tbsp	2 tbsp
Ground ginger	5 ml	1 tsp	1 tsp
Lemon juice	5 ml	1 tsp	1 tsp

1. Trim roots and tops off spring onions, make several cuts through white bulb to a depth of about 2.5 cm/ 1 in. Place in a bowl of cold water in the fridge.

2. Cut cucumber into thin strips. Place in a serving bowl and chill.

3. Put turkey in a shallow dish. Mix marinade ingredients together and pour over. Leave to stand for at least 1 hour.

4. Mix plum jam with the soy sauce, ginger and lemon juice. Put in a small serving bowl. Warm tortillas either on a covered plate over a pan of boiling water or in the microwave.

5. Heat oil in a large frying pan (skillet). Drain turkey and stir-fry for about 5 minutes until cooked through. Turn into a serving dish.

6. To serve: take a tortilla, use a spring onion 'brush' to dip in plum sauce and spread sauce over tortilla. Add a spoonful of meat and some cucumber. Roll up and eat with the fingers.

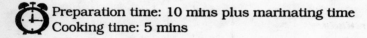 Preparation time: 10 mins plus marinating time
Cooking time: 5 mins

ORIENTAL CHICKEN LOAF

Serves 4–6	Metric	Imperial	American
Cooked minced (ground) chicken	350 g	12 oz	12 oz
Onion, minced	75 g	3 oz	³/₄ cup
Can crushed pineapple, drained	440 g	15¹/₂ oz	15¹/₂ oz
Canned pimiento cap, chopped	1	1	1
Soy sauce	15 ml	1 tbsp	1 tbsp
Packets bread sauce mix	2	2	2
Salt and pepper			
Eggs, beaten	2	2	2
To serve:			
Canned beansprouts with grated cucumber and carrot salad (oil, vinegar and soy sauce dressing)			

1. Mix all loaf ingredients together and place in a lightly greased loaf tin.

2. Cover with a double thickness of foil and steam for 1 hour. Leave to cool.

3. Turn out onto a serving dish and serve cold, cut into slices, with beansprouts, carrot and cucumber salad.

 Preparation time: 5 mins
Cooking time: 1 hour plus cooling time

CHEAT CHICKEN MARYLAND

Serves 4	Metric	Imperial	American
Chicken nuggets, crumb-coated	*450 g*	*1 lb*	*1 lb*
Streaky bacon rashers	*4-8*	*4-8*	*4-8*
Large bananas	*2*	*2*	*2*
Oil for frying			
Corn Fritters (page 32)			
To serve:			
New potatoes			
Green salad			

1. Grill (broil) or fry (sauté) chicken nuggets according to packet directions. Keep warm.

2. Cut bacon rashers in half, roll up and grill or fry until cooked through. Keep warm.

3. Cut bananas in half lengthwise then across to make 4 pieces. Fry in a little oil until just softening. Serve with the chicken, bacon, corn fritters, new potatoes and a green salad.

 Preparation time: 5 mins plus making corn fritters
Cooking time: 20 mins

CHICKEN AND VEGETABLE MORNAY

Substitute tuna for the chicken if preferred.

Serves 4	Metric	Imperial	American
Packet cheese sauce mix	1	1	1
Milk or water (according to packet)	300 ml	½ pt	1¼ cups
Cooked leftover vegetables, chopped (or frozen vegetables, cooked)	350 g	12 oz	3 cups
Cooked chicken	175 g	6 oz	1½ cups
Grated nutmeg	1.5 ml	¼ tsp	¼ tsp
Cheddar cheese, grated	50 g	2 oz	½ cup
To serve:			
Garlic bread (page 183)			

1. Make up cheese sauce according to packet directions.

2. Stir in vegetables, chicken and nutmeg. Heat through for 3 minutes, stirring occasionally.

3. Turn into a 1.2 L/2 pt/5 cup flameproof dish. Sprinkle with grated cheese and grill (broil) for 5 minutes until cheese is melted and turning golden. Serve hot with garlic bread.

Preparation time: 3 mins
Cooking time: about 10 mins

QUICK CASSOULET

Serves 4–6	Metric	Imperial	American
Bacon rashers (slices) or cooked ham slices, diced	4	4	4
Can hot dog sausages, drained and cut in pieces	400 g	14 oz	14 oz
Can red kidney beans, drained	425 g	15 oz	15 oz
Can baked beans in tomato sauce	425 g	15 oz	15 oz
Can cut green beans, drained	275 g	10 oz	10 oz
To serve:			
Crusty bread			

1. Dry-fry bacon, if using, in a large saucepan.

2. Stir in remaining ingredients. Heat through, occasionally stirring gently until piping hot, about 5 minutes. Serve in soup bowls with crusty bread.

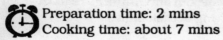
Preparation time: 2 mins
Cooking time: about 7 mins

BARBECUED BANGERS

Serves 4	Metric	Imperial	American
Chipolata sausages	450 g	1 lb	1 lb
Butter or margarine	15 g	1/2 oz	1 tbsp
Lemon juice	15 ml	1 tbsp	1 tbsp
Red wine vinegar	15 ml	1 tbsp	1 tbsp
Tomato purée (paste)	30 ml	2 tbsp	2 tbsp
Brown table sauce	15 ml	1 tbsp	1 tbsp
Golden (light corn) syrup	30 ml	2 tbsp	2 tbsp
To serve:			
Boiled rice			
Peas			

1. Dry-fry sausages in a large frying pan (skillet) until cooked through and brown all over (about 10 minutes).

2. Heat remaining ingredients together in a saucepan. Pour over sausages and cook for a further 3 minutes until sausages are coated in a sticky sauce.

3. Serve with boiled rice and peas.

 Preparation time: 2 mins
Cooking time: 13 mins

SAUERKRAUT WITH FRANKFURTERS

Serves 4	Metric	Imperial	American
Jar sauerkraut	*1*	*1*	*1*
Caraway seeds	*15 ml*	*1 tbsp*	*1 tbsp*
Vacuum-packed or canned			
frankfurters	*12*	*12*	*12*
To serve:			
Plain boiled potatoes			
German or Dijon mustard			

1. Empty sauerkraut into a saucepan. Add caraway seeds and heat through. Drain.

2. Heat frankfurters according to packet directions.

3. Serve on hot plates with plain boiled potatoes and mustard.

 Preparation time: 4 mins
Cooking time: 8 mins

SAUSAGE SALAD

Serves 4–6	Metric	Imperial	American
White bread slices, cubed	4	4	4
Oil	45 ml	3 tbsp	3 tbsp
Thick sausages, cooked and sliced	8	8	8
Cans mexicorn (corn with (bell) peppers), drained	2 x 300 g	2 x 11 oz	2 x 11 oz
Can butter beans, drained	425 g	15 oz	15 oz
Cucumber, diced	$1/2$	$1/2$	$1/2$
Bunch of radishes, trimmed and quartered (optional)	1	1	1
Garlic clove, crushed	1	1	1
Plain yoghurt or soured (dairy sour) cream	150 ml	$1/4$ pt	$1/3$ cup
Dried chives	15 ml	1 tbsp	1 tbsp

1. Fry (sauté) cubes of bread in the hot oil until golden. Drain on kitchen paper.

2. Mix sausages with corn, butter beans, cucumber and radishes, if using. Chill until ready to serve.

3. Mix garlic with yoghurt or soured cream and chives. Chill.

4. Just before serving, add the fried bread to the salad and toss. Pile onto serving plates and add a spoonful of the creamy dressing on top. Serve immediately.

 Preparation time: 10 mins plus chilling
Cooking time: (if necessary for sausages) 10 mins

SMOKED CHEESE AND FRANKFURTER FLAN

Serves 4–6	Metric	Imperial	American
Shortcrust pastry (basic pie crust)	225 g	8 oz	1/2 lb
Filling:			
Onion, chopped	1	1	1
Oil	15 ml	1 tbsp	1 tbsp
Can chopped tomatoes	225 g	8 oz	8 oz
Cinnamon	2.5 ml	1/2 tsp	1/2 tsp
Tomato purée (paste)	15 ml	1 tbsp	1 tbsp
Frankfurters (can or vacuum packed)	5	5	5
Smoked cheese roll	100 g	4 oz	1/4 lb
To serve:			
Salad			
Jacket potatoes			

1. Roll out pastry. Line a 23 cm/9 in flan dish (pie pan). Prick base with a fork, line with crumpled foil and bake 'blind' for 10 minutes. Remove foil and return to oven for 5 minutes to dry out.

2. Meanwhile fry (sauté) onion in the oil for 3 minutes until soft but not brown. Add tomatoes, cinnamon and tomato purée and simmer for 10 minutes. Chop frankfurters, add to sauce and turn into flan case (pie shell).

3. Slice cheese and arrange in a ring around top.

4. Bake in oven at 190°C/375°F/gas mark 5 for 15 minutes until cheese is golden and flan is hot through. Serve hot or cold with salad and jacket potatoes.

Preparation time: 5 mins
Cooking time: 38 mins plus pastry drying out time

HAM IN PUFF PASTRY

Serves 6	Metric	Imperial	American
Frozen puff pastry (paste), *thawed*	*450 g*	*1 lb*	*1 lb*
Cans of ham	*2 x 450 g*	*2 x 1 lb*	*2 x 1 lb*
Can creamed mushrooms	*215 g*	*7¹/₂ oz*	*7¹/₂ oz*
Dried marjoram or oregano	*10 ml*	*2 tsp*	*2 tsp*
Egg, beaten, to glaze			
Cumberland sauce:			
Redcurrant jelly (clear *conserve)*	*45 ml*	*3 tbsp*	*3 tbsp*
Orange juice	*45 ml*	*3 tbsp*	*3 tbsp*
To garnish:			
Parsley, if available			
To serve:			
New potatoes			
Green beans			

1.   Cut pastry into 6 equal pieces and roll out each piece to a square about 18-20 cm/7-8 in. Trim edges.

2.   Cut each can of ham into three slices, discarding jelly.

3.   Divide can of mushrooms between centres of pastry. Sprinkle with herbs then top each with a slice of ham.

4.   Brush edges of pastry with beaten egg. Fold over filling to form parcels.

5.   Place parcels, folds down, on a dampened baking sheet. Make 'leaves' out of pastry trimmings and place on parcels. Brush with beaten egg to glaze.

6.   Bake in a hot oven 220°C/425°F/gas mark 7 for 12-15 minutes until golden brown.

7. Meanwhile, heat redcurrant jelly (clear conserve) with the orange juice in a saucepan until it has dissolved.

8. Transfer ham parcels to warm serving plates, spoon a little sauce to the side of each and garnish with parsley. Serve hot with potatoes and green beans.

Preparation time: 15 mins
Cooking time: 12-15 mins

GRILLED HAM WITH PINEAPPLE

Serves 4	Metric	Imperial	American
Can ham	450 g	1 lb	1 lb
Can chopped tomatoes, drained	225 g	8 oz	8 oz
Cheddar cheese, grated	75 g	3 oz	3/4 cup
Can pineapple slices	225 g	8 oz	8 oz
To serve:			
French fries			
Peas			

1. Cut ham into four steaks, discarding jelly. Place on a grill (broiler) pan and grill (broil) for 1 minute. Turn over and grill other side for a further minute.

2. Spoon drained tomatoes over and top with grated cheese and place a pineapple slice on each.

3. Return to grill and cook until bubbling, hot through and top is turning golden. Serve hot with French fries and peas.

Preparation time: 2 mins
Cooking time: 7 mins

Orange Glazed Ham Steaks

Serves 4	Metric	Imperial	American
Can ham	450 g	1 lb	1 lb
Butter or margarine	15 g	1/2 oz	1 tbsp
Orange marmalade, fine shred	30 ml	2 tbsp	2 tbsp
Ground ginger	2.5 ml	1/2 tsp	1/2 tsp
Lemon juice	5 ml	1 tsp	1 tsp
To serve:			
Creamed potatoes			
Mushrooms			
Tomatoes			

1. Cut ham into four steaks, discarding jelly.

2. Melt butter or margarine in a frying pan (skillet) and fry (sauté) ham for 2 minutes. Turn over.

3. Mix marmalade, ginger and lemon juice together and spoon mixture all over steaks.

4. Cook for about 3 minutes, basting with the glaze. Place pan under a pre-heated grill (broiler) for 2 minutes until meat is stickily glazed. Serve hot with creamed potatoes, mushrooms and tomatoes.

 Preparation time: 2 mins
Cooking time: 7 mins

VEGETARIAN MEALS

You don't have to be a whole-hearted vegetarian to enjoy meatless meals. All the following are tasty, nutritious dishes for all the family.

STUFFED PIZZAS

Serves 4	Metric	Imperial	American
Pizza base mixes	2	2	2
Can creamed mushrooms	215 g	7½ oz	7½ oz
Can chopped tomatoes, drained	225 g	8 oz	8 oz
Canned pimiento cap, chopped (optional)	1	1	1
Capers	5 ml	1 tsp	1 tsp
Cooked peas or green beans	15 ml	1 tbsp	1 tbsp
Mozzarella or Cheddar cheese, grated			
To garnish:			
Passata (or sieved canned tomatoes)			
Parmesan cheese, grated			

1. Make up pizza mixes according to packet directions.

2. Knead gently and cut into quarters. Roll out each piece, or flatten between the hands to rounds about 20 cm/8 in in diameter.

3. Divide all the filling ingredients between centres of each round of dough. Brush edges with water and draw up over filling to seal.

4. Place on a lightly greased baking sheet, sealed sides down.

5. Bake in a hot oven 200°C/400°F/gas mark 6 for about 20 minutes or until golden brown.

6. Transfer to warm serving plates. Spoon a little hot passata over, sprinkle with Parmesan cheese and serve.

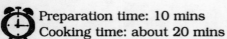
Preparation time: 10 mins
Cooking time: about 20 mins

PASTA SURPRISE

Serves 4	Metric	Imperial	American
Pasta shapes	225 g	8 oz	2 cups
Passata (or sieved canned tomatoes)	300 ml	1/2 pt	1 1/4 cups
Can sweetcorn (corn)	200 g	7 oz	7 oz
Dried oregano	2.5 ml	1/2 tsp	1/2 tsp
Salt and pepper			
Frozen chopped spinach	225 g	8 oz	1 cup
Packet cheese sauce mix	1	1	1
Milk or water (according to packet)	300 ml	1/2 pt	1 1/4 cups
Cheddar or Parmesan cheese, grated (optional)	50 g	2 oz	1/2 cup

1. Cook pasta according to packet directions. Drain, stir in passata, sweetcorn, oregano and seasoning and heat through.

2. Cook spinach according to packet directions, drain if necessary.

3. Make up cheese sauce according to packet directions.

4. Put half the pasta mixture into base of a 1.5 L/2½ pt/ 6 cup fireproof dish. Top with spinach then rest of pasta.

5. Spoon sauce over, cover with grated cheese, if using and brown under a hot grill (broiler) for about 5 minutes. Serve hot.

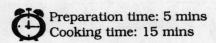 Preparation time: 5 mins
Cooking time: 15 mins

EGG AND VEGETABLE PLATTER

Serves 4	Metric	Imperial	American
Cooked left-over vegetables including potatoes (or cooked frozen vegetables and a little prepared instant mash)	350 g	12 oz	3 cups
Pepper			
Butter	15 g	1/2 oz	1 tbsp
Brown table sauce	15 ml	1 tbsp	1 tbsp
Eggs	4	4	4
Oil			

1. Chop vegetables. Season lightly with pepper. Melt butter in a large frying pan (skillet) and add half the vegetables. Press down flat.

2. Spread the brown sauce over the top with rest of vegetables, again pressing down well.

3. Cover with a plate and cook gently for about 15 minutes. Then loosen base and turn out onto plate. Cut in quarters.

4. Meanwhile fry eggs in the oil (or poach in water). Slide one egg on top of each cake and serve hot.

 Preparation time: 3 mins
Cooking time: 15 mins

SAVOURY EGGY RICE

Serves 2–4	Metric	Imperial	American
Packet savoury rice	1	1	1
Eggs	4	4	4
To serve:			
Garlic bread (page 183)			

1. Empty packet of rice into a large frying pan (skillet).
    Add water as directed on the packet and bring to the
    boil. Cover with a lid and simmer for 15 minutes.

2. Remove lid, stir, make four 'wells' in rice mixture,
    break an egg into each, cover and continue cooking
    over a gentle heat for 5 minutes or until eggs are set.
    Serve straight from the pan with garlic bread.

Preparation time: 2 mins
Cooking time: 20 mins

BROCCOLI AND CIDER CHEESE

Serves 4	Metric	Imperial	American
Frozen broccoli	350 g	12 oz	3 cups
Packet cheese sauce mix	1	1	1
Cider	300 ml	1/2 pt	1 1/4 cups
Cheddar cheese, grated	50 g	2 oz	1/2 cup
To serve:			
Grilled (broiled) tomatoes			
Crusty bread			

1. Cook broccoli according to packet directions. Drain
    and arrange in a fairly shallow flameproof dish.

2. Make up cheese sauce using cider instead of milk.
    Pour over broccoli and top with grated cheese.

3. Place under a hot grill (broiler) until golden brown and
    bubbling (about 5 minutes). Serve with grilled tomatoes
    and crusty bread.

Preparation time: 2 mins
Cooking time: 10 mins

SPINACH AND MUSHROOM ROLL

Serves 4	Metric	Imperial	American
Frozen spinach, thawed	300 g	11 oz	1¹/₃ cups
Grated nutmeg	pinch	pinch	pinch
Eggs, separated	4	4	4
Salt and pepper			
Can creamed mushrooms	215 g	7¹/₂ oz	7¹/₂ oz
To serve:			
Hot passata or Quick Tomato Sauce (page 177)			
Buttered noodles			

1. Grease and line an 18 x 28 cm/7 x 11 in Swiss (jelly) roll tin and line with baking parchment.

2. Cook spinach according to packet directions, drain well. Add nutmeg and egg yolks and beat well. Season with a little salt and pepper.

3. Whisk egg whites until stiff. Fold into spinach with a metal spoon. Turn into prepared tin.

4. Bake in a hot oven 200°C/400°F/gas mark 6 for 20 minutes or until just firm to the touch.

5. Heat creamed mushrooms.

6. Turn spinach mixture out onto a clean sheet of baking parchment. Quickly spread with creamed mushrooms and roll up using baking parchment to help.

7. Transfer to a serving plate and serve with hot passata or tomato sauce and buttered noodles.

Preparation time: 10 mins
Cooking time: 25 mins

THE FASTEST SOUFFLÉ IN THE WEST

Serves 4	Metric	Imperial	American
Butter, for greasing			
Can sliced mushrooms, drained	300 g	11 oz	11 oz
Can condensed cream of mushroom soup	295 g	10½ oz	10½ oz
Cheddar or Parmesan (or half and half) cheese, grated	75 g	3 oz	¾ cup
Eggs, separated	4	4	4
Black pepper			
To serve:			
Salad			

1. Grease an 18 cm/7 in soufflé dish with the butter.

2. Put drained mushrooms in base of dish.

3. Empty soup into a bowl. Whisk in cheese and egg yolks. Season with pepper.

4. Whisk egg whites until stiff. Fold into mixture with a metal spoon.

5. Turn into dish and bake in a hot oven 200°C/400°F/ gas mark 6 for 25-30 minutes until risen, golden and just set. Serve immediately with a salad.

Variations:

Use any combination you like:
Drained asparagus tips with asparagus soup
Baked beans, ratatouille or cut celery with celery soup
Sweetcorn (corn) with chicken soup (not for vegetarians!)

 Preparation time: 4 mins
Cooking time: 25-30 mins

BEAN STEW WITH DUMPLINGS

Serves 4–6	Metric	Imperial	American
Can butter beans, drained	425 g	15 oz	15 oz
Can black-eyed beans, drained	425 g	15 oz	15 oz
Can chopped tomatoes	400 g	14 oz	14 oz
Garlic clove, crushed	1	1	1
Tomato purée (paste)	15 ml	1 tbsp	1 tbsp
Can sweetcorn (corn) with (bell) peppers	200 g	7 oz	7 oz
Can cut green beans	275 g	10 oz	10 oz
Vegetable stock	300 ml	1/2 pt	1 1/4 cups
Bay leaf	1	1	1
Salt and pepper			
Packet dumpling mix	1	1	1
Cheddar cheese, grated	50 g	2 oz	1/2 cup
Dried mixed herbs			

1. Empty drained butter and black-eyed beans into a saucepan with the tomatoes, garlic, tomato purée, contents of cans of sweetcorn and green beans (not drained), stock, bay leaf and a little salt and pepper. Bring to the boil, reduce heat, cover and simmer for 5 minutes. Discard bay leaf.

2. Meanwhile empty dumpling mix into a bowl with the cheese and herbs. Add enough cold water to form a soft, but not sticky dough. Shape into 8 balls.

3. Arrange dumplings around top of stew, cover and simmer for 15-20 minutes until fluffy. Serve hot.

Preparation time: 4 mins
Cooking time: 20-25 mins

OMELETTE IN THE FINGERS

Serves 2–4	Metric	Imperial	American
Eggs	*4*	*4*	*4*
Cold water	*60 ml*	*4 tbsp*	*4 tbsp*
Salt and pepper			
Mixed dried herbs	*5 ml*	*1 tsp*	*1 tsp*
Butter			
Can asparagus spears, drained	*290 g*	*10½ oz*	*10½ oz*
To serve:			
Crusty bread			
Chunky salad pieces			

1. Beat one egg into a bowl with 15 ml/1 tbsp water, a little salt and pepper and 1.5 ml/¼ tsp herbs.

2. Heat a little butter in an omelette pan. Pour in egg and fry (sauté), lifting edge and letting uncooked egg run underneath until set. Transfer to a plate and leave to cool while making remaining three omelettes in the same way.

3. Divide asparagus spears amongst omelettes. Roll up and serve with crusty bread and chunky salad pieces that can be eaten in the fingers.

 Preparation time: 2 mins
Cooking time: about 10 mins plus cooling time

WALDORF GRILL

Serves 4	Metric	Imperial	American
Can celery hearts	515 g	18¹/₂ oz	18¹/₂ oz
Eating (dessert) apple, thinly sliced	1	1	1
Packet cheese sauce mix	1	1	1
Milk or water (according to packet)	300 ml	¹/₂ pt	1¹/₄ cups
Walnut pieces, chopped	50 g	2 oz	¹/₂ cup
Cheddar cheese, grated	50 g	2 oz	¹/₂ cup
To serve:			
Jacket potatoes			

1. Empty celery into a flameproof casserole (Dutch oven). Add apple slices. Bring to the boil, simmer for 2 minutes then drain off liquid.

2. Meanwhile make up cheese sauce according to packet directions. Stir in walnuts.

3. Pour sauce over celery and apple. Cover with grated cheese. Place under a hot grill (broiler) for about 5 minutes until golden and bubbling. Serve hot with jacket potatoes.

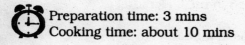

Preparation time: 3 mins
Cooking time: about 10 mins

FLUFFY CHEESE PUDDING

Serves 4	Metric	Imperial	American
Butter	*25 g*	*1 oz*	*2 tbsp*
Eggs, separated	*2*	*2*	*2*
Milk	*300 ml*	*¹/₂ pt*	*1¹/₄ cups*
Breadcrumbs, fresh	*75 g*	*3 oz*	*1¹/₂ cups*
Cheddar cheese, grated	*100 g*	*4 oz*	*1 cup*
Salt and pepper			
To serve:			
Baked fresh or canned			
tomatoes			

1. Grease a 1.2 L/2 pt/5 cup ovenproof dish well with the butter.

2. Beat egg yolks with milk and stir in the breadcrumbs, cheese and a little salt and pepper. Leave to stand for 15 minutes.

3. Whisk egg whites until stiff and fold into mixture with a metal spoon. Turn into prepared dish.

4. Cook in a hot oven 200°C/400°F/gas mark 6 for 35 minutes until risen and golden. Serve immediately with baked fresh or canned tomatoes.

 Preparation time: 3 mins plus standing time
Cooking time: 35 mins

MIXED VEGETABLE FRITTERS WITH GARLIC MAYONNAISE

Serves 4	Metric	Imperial	American
Garlic Mayonnaise:			
Garlic cloves, crushed	*3*	*3*	*3*
Mayonnaise	*150 ml*	*1/4 pt*	*2/3 cup*
Black pepper and salt			
Fritters:			
Plain (all-purpose) flour	*75 g*	*3 oz*	*3/4 cup*
Tepid water	*120 ml*	*4 fl oz*	*1/2 cup*
Oil	*15 ml*	*1 tbsp*	*1 tbsp*
Can mixed vegetables, drained	*275 g*	*10 oz*	*10 oz*
Egg white	*1*	*1*	*1*
Oil for deep frying			

1. Mix garlic with the mayonnaise and a little seasoning. Cover well and chill until ready to serve.

2. To make fritters, mix flour with the water and oil until smooth. Stir in well-drained vegetables.

3. Whisk egg white until stiff and fold into batter with a metal spoon.

4. Heat oil until a cube of day-old bread browns in 30 seconds. Deep fry spoonfuls of the mixture, a few at a time until crisp and golden. Drain on kitchen paper and serve hot with the chilled garlic sauce.

Preparation time: 5 mins
Cooking time: about 20 mins

STUFFED CABBAGE LEAVES

A great way to use up the outer leaves of cabbage you'd usually throw away!

Serves 4	Metric	Imperial	American
Cabbage leaves, large	8	8	8
Can ratatouille	425 g	15 oz	15 oz
Cooked long-grain rice	60 ml	4 tbsp	4 tbsp
Vegetable stock	300 ml	½ pt	1¼ cups
Passata (or sieved tomatoes)	45 ml	3 tbsp	3 tbsp
Salt and pepper			
To serve:			
Cheddar cheese, grated			
Crusty bread			

1. Cut out thick central base stalk from leaves.

2. Put leaves in a pan of boiling water and cook for 3-4 minutes to soften. Drain, rinse with cold water and drain again.

3. Mix ratatouille with the rice.

4. Dry leaves with kitchen paper. Lay upside down on a board. Overlap the two points where stalk was. Put a good spoonful of filling on top. Fold in sides then roll up.

5. Pack into the base of a lightly greased heavy flameproof casserole (Dutch oven).

6. Mix stock with passata and pour over. Sprinkle with a little salt and pepper. Bring to the boil, reduce heat, cover and simmer for 20 minutes or until cabbage is tender.

7. Serve hot with grated cheese and crusty bread.

Preparation time: 3 mins
Cooking time: 24 mins

DESSERTS

No meal is complete unless it is rounded off with something sweet, exciting and utterly delicious. Well, now you can do tons better than the chill cabinet at the supermarket – there's a whole range of fantastic desserts just waiting to burst out of your pantry! Some of the best ideas are the simplest. To create a Chocolate Orange Sundae in minutes, stir 60 ml/4 tbsp of chocolate spread into 300 ml/ ^{1}/$_2$ pt/1^1/$_4$ cups of whipped cream then layer it into wine goblets with a can of drained mandarin oranges. Chill and serve sprinkled with a few toasted nuts. Now for a whole host more ideas...

CHOCOLATE RIPPLE RING

Serves 6	Metric	Imperial	American
Chocolate hazelnut spread	45 ml	3 tbsp	3 tbsp
Coffee liqueur	30 ml	2 tbsp	2 tbsp
Soft scoop chocolate ice cream	1 L	1³/₄ pts	4¹/₄ cups
To decorate:			
Whipped cream			
Grated chocolate			

1. Blend chocolate spread with the liqueur until smooth.

2. Turn ice cream into a bowl. Mash with a fork then quickly fold in chocolate mixture to form ripples.

3. Pack into a 1 L/1³/₄ pt/4¹/₄ cup ring mould (mold). Wrap and freeze until firm.

4. Dip base of mould in hot water then loosen edge with a warmed knife. Turn out onto a serving plate and decorate with whipped cream in centre and grated chocolate.

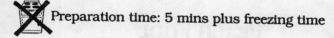 Preparation time: 5 mins plus freezing time

THE UBIQUITOUS TRIFLE

Serves 4	Metric	Imperial	American
Trifle sponges	4	4	4
Can strawberries	300 g	11 oz	11 oz
Sherry	30 ml	2 tbsp	2 tbsp
Can custard	425 g	15 oz	15 oz
Whipped cream	150 ml	¼ pt	⅔ cup
To decorate:			
Flaked almonds			

1. Crumble sponge cakes into base of a glass serving dish.

2. Empty contents of can of strawberries over and crush well. Sprinkle sherry over top.

3. Spoon on custard then spread lightly whipped cream on top. Sprinkle with almonds and chill until ready to serve.

 Preparation time: 3 mins plus chilling time

PEACH FOOL

Serves 4	Metric	Imperial	American
Can peach slices, drained reserving juice	410 g	14½ oz	14½ oz
Can custard	425 g	15 oz	15 oz
Plain yoghurt	150 ml	¼ pt	⅔ cup
To decorate:			
Glacé (candied) cherries			

1. Liquidise or purée peaches in a food processor.

2. Fold in custard until well blended.

3. Fold in yoghurt until there is a marbled effect.

4. Spoon into glasses. Chill. Top each with a glacé cherry and a little of the reserved juice just before serving.

 Preparation time: 3 mins plus chilling time

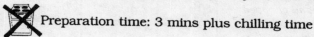

THE BEST CUSTARD TART

Serve 4–6	Metric	Imperial	American
Shortcrust pastry (basic pie crust)	*175 g*	*6 oz*	*¹/₃ lb*
Eggs	*2*	*2*	*2*
Milk	*150 ml*	*¹/₄ pt*	*²/₃ cup*
Can custard	*425 g*	*15 oz*	*15 oz*
Caster (superfine) sugar	*25 g*	*1 oz*	*2 tbsp*
Grated nutmeg			

1. Roll out pastry and use to line a 20 cm/8 in flan dish (pie pan) set on a baking sheet.

2. Beat eggs with milk then stir in remaining ingredients except nutmeg. Pour into flan case (pie shell).

3. Sprinkle a little nutmeg over, then bake in a moderately hot oven 190°C/375°F/gas mark 5 for about 40 minutes or until set. Serve warm or cold.

Preparation time: 5 mins
Cooking time: 40 mins

ITALIAN CASSATA

Serves 6	Metric	Imperial	American
Soft scoop vanilla ice cream	1 L	1¾ pts	4¼ cups
Grated chocolate	50 g	2 oz	½ cup
Jar maraschino cherries, drained and chopped	50 g	2 oz	½ cup
To decorate:			
Maraschino cherry			

1. Put ice cream into a bowl. Quickly mash in chocolate and cherries until just blended. Don't overmix or ice cream will start to melt.

2. Pack into a 1 L/1¾ pt/4¼ cup pudding basin, cover and freeze until firm.

3. To serve, loosen edge with a knife warmed under hot water. Turn out onto a serving plate, put a cherry on top and serve straight away.

 Preparation time: 5 mins plus freezing time

HONEY NUT BOMB

Serves 6	Metric	Imperial	American
Soft scoop vanilla ice cream	1 L	1¾ pts	4¼ cups
Lemon, grated rind and juice	1	1	1
Clear honey	45 ml	3 tbsp	3 tbsp
Toasted nuts, chopped	50 g	2 oz	½ cup
To decorate:			
Crystallised (candied) lemon slices			

1. Put ice cream into a bowl. Quickly fold in the lemon rind and juice, honey and nuts to give a marbled effect. Don't overmix or ice cream will melt.

2. Pack into a 1 L/1¾ pt/4¼ cup pudding basin. Cover and freeze until firm.

3. Loosen edge with a knife warmed under hot water, turn out and serve straight away decorated with crystallised lemon slices.

 Preparation time: 5 mins plus freezing time

CARIBBEAN COOLER

Serves 6	Metric	Imperial	American
Soft scoop chocolate ice cream	*1 L*	*1¾ pts*	*4¼ cups*
Bananas, mashed with lemon juice	*2*	*2*	*2*
Crystallised or stem ginger	*25 g*	*1 oz*	*2 tbsp*
To decorate:			
Grated chocolate			

1. Put ice cream into a bowl. Quickly work in bananas and ginger until just mixed. Don't overmix or ice cream will start to melt.

2. Pack into a 450 g/1 lb loaf tin. Wrap and freeze until firm.

3. To serve, stand base of tin in hot water briefly. Loosen edge with a knife and turn out. Decorate with grated chocolate and serve cut in slices.

 Preparation time: 5 mins plus freezing time

RUM AND RAISIN MOUNTAIN

Serves 6	Metric	Imperial	American
Raisins	50 g	2 oz	$^1/_3$ cup
Rum	30 ml	2 tbsp	2 tbsp
Meringues, crushed	2-3	2-3	2-3
Soft scoop vanilla ice cream	1 L	1$^3/_4$ pt	4$^1/_4$ cups
To decorate:			
Whipped cream			

1. Put raisins in a bowl. Add rum and leave to soak for at least 1 hour.

2. Mash soaked raisins into the ice cream with the crushed meringues. Work quickly to prevent the ice cream from melting.

3. Pack into a 1 L/1¾ pt/4¼ cup pudding basin. Cover and freeze until firm.

4. Loosen edge with a warmed knife. Turn out onto a serving plate and pile whipped cream on top. Serve immediately.

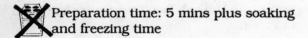 Preparation time: 5 mins plus soaking and freezing time

MOCK RUM BABAS

Serves 6	Metric	Imperial	American
Granulated sugar	100 g	4 oz	¹/₂ cup
Water	150 ml	¹/₄ pt	²/₃ cup
Rum or rum essence (extract) and water	30 ml	2 tbsp	2 tbsp
Ring doughnuts	6	6	6
Whipped cream			
Chopped nuts			

1. Dissolve sugar in the water. Boil for 5 minutes until syrupy.

2. Stir in the rum.

3. Prick doughnuts all over with a skewer and spoon rum syrup over them. Leave to soak in well.

4. Fill centres with whipped cream, decorate with nuts and chill, if time, before serving.

 Preparation time: 2 mins
Cooking time: 5 mins plus chilling time

FRUIT PARCELS

Makes about 8	Metric	Imperial	American
Filo pastry sheets (approx)	8	8	8
Butter, melted	75 g	3 oz	$^1/_3$ cup
Can peach or pear halves	410 g	14$^1/_2$ oz	14$^1/_2$ oz
Jar mincemeat	450 g	1 lb	1 lb

1. For each parcel, brush a sheet of filo pastry with a little butter. Fold in half and brush again.

2. Place a peach or pear half in the centre of each pastry sheet and top with a spoonful of mincemeat. Reserve juice.

3. Draw pastry up over filling to form parcel. Transfer to a buttered baking sheet and brush pastry with a little more melted butter. Continue with the rest of the ingredients.

4. Bake in a hot oven 200°C/400°F/gas mark 6 for about 15 minutes until golden brown.

5. Serve hot or cold with a little of the reserved juice.

Preparation time: 10 mins
Cooking time: 15 mins

LEMON VELVET

Serves 4	Metric	Imperial	American
Packet lemon meringue pie filling mix	*1*	*1*	*1*
Water	*300 ml*	*¹/₂ pt*	*1¹/₄ cups*
Lemon, grated rind and juice (or a little bottled lemon juice)	*1*	*1*	*1*
Milk, cold	*150 ml*	*¹/₄ pt*	*²/₃ cup*
Packet Dream Topping mix	*1*	*1*	*1*
To decorate:			
Crystallised lemon slices			

1. Blend lemon meringue pie mix with water, bring to the boil, stirring until thickened. Stir in lemon rind and juice and leave to cool.

2. Put cold milk in a bowl. Add Dream Topping and whisk until thick and fluffy.

3. Fold into cold lemon mixture. Pile into 4 glasses and decorate each with a crystallised lemon slice before serving.

 Preparation time: 6 mins
Cooking time: 3 mins plus chilling time

CHOCOLATE CUPS

Serves 6	Metric	Imperial	American
Whipping cream	*150 ml*	*¹/₄ pt*	*²/₃ cup*
Chocolate hazelnut spread	*30 ml*	*2 tbsp*	*2 tbsp*
Brandy, sherry, rum or			
whisky	*15 ml*	*1 tbsp*	*1 tbsp*
Ready-made chocolate shells	*6*	*6*	*6*
To decorate:			
Toasted chopped hazelnuts			
or glacé (candied)			
cherries			
To serve:			
Any fresh or drained canned			
fruit			

1. Whip cream and fold in the chocolate spread and brandy, sherry, rum or whisky.

2. Spoon into chocolate cups and swirl tops with a teaspoon. Alternatively put mixture into a piping bag and pipe it into cases.

3. Sprinkle with chopped nuts or add a halved glacé cherry to each. Chill until ready to serve.

4. Place on serving plates and arrange slices of fruit attractively at the side of each cup.

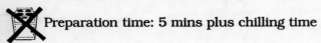 Preparation time: 5 mins plus chilling time

ALMOST TIRAMISU

Serves 6	Metric	Imperial	American
Trifle sponges	*4*	*4*	*4*
Strong black coffee	*150 ml*	*¹/₄ pt*	*²/₃ cup*
Packet egg custard (or crème caramel) mix	*1*	*1*	*1*
Milk	*450 ml*	*³/₄ pt*	*2 cups*
Brandy or coffee liqueur	*15-30 ml*	*1-2 tbsp*	*1-2 tbsp*
Whipped cream	*150 ml*	*¹/₄ pt*	*²/₃ cup*
Drinking chocolate (sweetened chocolate) powder	*15 ml*	*1 tbsp*	*1 tbsp*

1. Break up the sponges and place in a shallow round glass dish.

2. Add the coffee and leave to soak.

3. Make up the egg custard or crème caramel mix with the milk. Leave to cool slightly, then stir in brandy or coffee liqueur.

4. Carefully pour over the sponge and chill until set.

5. Cover with whipped cream and dust with chocolate powder.

Note:

If you use crème caramel mix, reserve the sachet of caramel to drizzle over yoghurt and fresh bananas as another dessert.

 Preparation time: 5 mins plus chilling time

COFFEE NUT DELIGHT

Serves 3–4	Metric	Imperial	American
Packet egg custard (or crème caramel) mix	*1*	*1*	*1*
Instant coffee powder	*15 ml*	*1 tbsp*	*1 tbsp*
Milk	*600 ml*	*1 pt*	*2¹/₂ cups*
Small packet peanut brittle	*1*	*1*	*1*
Thick plain yoghurt or fromage frais	*150 ml*	*¹/₄ pt*	*²/₃ cup*

1. Whisk custard mix and coffee into the milk. Bring to the boil and boil for 2 minutes as directed.

2. Cool slightly then pour into a glass serving dish. Leave to cool completely, then chill until set.

3. Put peanut brittle in a bag and crush it with a rolling pin.

4. Just before serving, spread yoghurt or fromage frais over coffee custard and sprinkle with the crushed peanut brittle.

Note:

If you used a crème caramel mix, drizzle the sachet of caramel over the yoghurt or fromage frais before adding peanut brittle.

Preparation time: 5 mins plus chilling

NO EFFORT CRUMBLE

Serves 3–4	Metric	Imperial	American
Can fruit, drained reserving juice	*410 g*	*14¹/₂ oz*	*14¹/₂ oz*
Weetabix	*2*	*2*	*2*
Demerara (light brown) sugar	*15 ml*	*1 tbsp*	*1 tbsp*
Butter or margarine, melted	*50 g*	*2 oz*	*¹/₄ cup*
Ground ginger, cinnamon or mixed (apple pie) spice	*2.5 ml*	*¹/₂ tsp*	*¹/₂ tsp*
To serve:			
Cream or custard			

1. Put fruit in a 1 L/1¾ pt/4¼ cup ovenproof dish.

2. Crumble cereal and mix with sugar, butter or margarine and spice.

3. Sprinkle over fruit, pressing down lightly. Bake in a moderately hot oven 190°C/375°F/gas mark 5 for about 15 minutes until crisp. Serve warm with cream or custard.

Preparation time: 3 mins
Cooking time: 15 mins

PEACH AND RAISIN CRISP

Serves 6	Metric	Imperial	American
Cans peach slices, drained,			
reserving juice	*2 x 410 g*	*2 x 14¹/₂ oz*	*2 x 14¹/₂ oz*
Raisins	*75 g*	*3 oz*	*¹/₂ cup*
Margarine	*25 g*	*1 oz*	*2 tbsp*
Plain (all-purpose) flour	*50 g*	*2 oz*	*¹/₂ cup*
Caster (superfine) sugar	*25 g*	*1 oz*	*2 tbsp*
Original Oat Crunch cereal	*100 g*	*4 oz*	*1 cup*
To serve:			
Custard			

1. Put fruit in the base of a 1.2 L/2 pt/5 cup ovenproof dish. Sprinkle raisins over.

2. Rub fat into the flour until mixture resembles breadcrumbs. Stir in the sugar and Original Oat Crunch. Spoon crumble over fruit and press down lightly.

3. Bake at 190°C/375°F/gas mark 5 for about 35 minutes until golden and crisp. Serve hot with custard and reserved juice.

⏰ Preparation time: 5 mins
Cooking time: 35 mins

PEACH MELBA MERINGUES

Serves 6	Metric	Imperial	American
Meringue nests	6	6	6
Low fat soft cheese	200 g	7 oz	scant 1 cup
Can peach halves, drained	410 g	14½ oz	14½ oz
Can raspberries	300 g	11 oz	11 oz

1. Put nests on 6 serving plates. Spoon a little soft cheese into each and spread gently.

2. Top each with a drained peach half, rounded side up.

3. Drain raspberries, sieve fruit. Thin to a pouring consistency with a little of the juice.

4. Just before serving, drizzle a little raspberry purée attractively over each filled meringue nest so it runs down onto the plate.

Preparation time: 5 mins

APRICOT AND GINGER FLAN

Serves 4	Metric	Imperial	American
Gingernuts (cookies), crushed	175 g	6 oz	1½ cups
Butter, melted	50 g	2 oz	¼ cup
Can apricot pie filling	½	½	½
Can evaporated milk, chilled	175 g	6 oz	6 oz
To decorate:			
Glacé (candied) cherries			
Angelica 'leaves'			

1. Mix biscuit crumbs with the butter and press into the base and sides of an 18 cm/7 in flan dish (pie pan). Chill until firm.

2. Sieve or liquidise pie filling to form a smooth purée.

3. Whip evaporated milk until thick and fluffy. Gradually whisk in the purée and spoon into flan case (pie pan).

4. Decorate with cherries and angelica and chill until ready to serve.

Note:

Sieve or liquidise the remaining pie filling, then heat it through with 15 ml/1 tbsp of orange liqueur or apricot brandy and serve spooned over vanilla ice cream for another dessert.

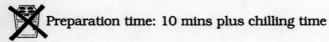 Preparation time: 10 mins plus chilling time

APRICOT NUT CRUNCH

Serves 6	Metric	Imperial	American
Can apricots	410 g	14¹/₂ oz	14¹/₂ oz
Orange jelly (jello) tablet	1	1	1
Butter	25 g	1 oz	2 tbsp
Golden (light corn) syrup	15 ml	1 tbsp	1 tbsp
Chopped nuts	15 ml	1 tbsp	1 tbsp
Corn or bran flakes	50 g	2 oz	2 cups
Thick plain yoghurt or whipped cream	150 ml	¹/₄ pt	²/₃ cup

1. Drain fruit, reserving juice. Sieve or liquidise fruit.

2. Make juice up to 450 ml/¾ pt/2 cups with water. Dissolve jelly tablet in a little of this liquid. Stir in remainder.

3. Stir in fruit purée and turn into a glass dish. Chill to set.

4. Melt butter with the syrup. Add nuts and lightly crushed cereal. Mix gently. Spread yoghurt or cream on top of apricots. Top with cereal mixture and chill again until ready to serve.

 Preparation time: 10 mins plus chilling time

SUMMER PUDDING ALL YEAR!

Serves 6	Metric	Imperial	American
White bread, sliced with crusts removed	5-6	5-6	5-6
Packet frozen summer fruits, thawed	500 g	18 oz	18 oz
Caster (superfine) sugar	75 g	3 oz	1/3 cup
To serve:			
Yoghurt or whipped cream			

1. Line a 900 ml/1½ pt/3¾ cup pudding basin with bread.

2. Stew the fruit with the sugar for 3 minutes. Turn into basin. Top with remaining bread, cutting to fit so there are no gaps.

3. Stand basin on a plate, cover with a saucer and weigh down. Chill overnight.

4. Turn out and serve with yoghurt or cream.

Preparation time: 10 mins plus chilling time

BLACK FOREST RICE

Serves 4	Metric	Imperial	American
Can cherry pie filling	410 g	14½ oz	14½ oz
Can chocolate rice pudding	425 g	15 oz	15 oz
Can cream			
To decorate:			
Grated chocolate or drinking (sweetened) chocolate powder			

1. Layer cherry pie filling and chocolate rice in 4 glasses.

2. Drain whey off cream and pipe or spoon a swirl of cream on top of each.

3. Sprinkle with grated chocolate or drinking chocolate powder. Chill, if you have time, before serving.

 Preparation time: 3 mins

RASPBERRY BAKED ALASKA

Serves 4	Metric	Imperial	American
Jam Swiss (jelly) roll	*1*	*1*	*1*
Egg whites	*3*	*3*	*3*
Caster (superfine) sugar	*175 g*	*6 oz*	*³/4 cup*
Scoops raspberry ripple ice cream	*8*	*8*	*8*
To decorate:			
Glacé (candied) cherries	*6*	*6*	*6*
Angelica 'leaves'	*6*	*6*	*6*

1. Slice Swiss roll and arrange in a single layer on an ovenproof plate.

2. Whisk egg whites until stiff. Whisk in half the sugar and continue whisking until stiff and glossy. Fold in remaining sugar with a metal spoon.

3. Just before serving pile ice cream in a mound on top of Swiss roll. Cover completely with meringue. Decorate with cherries and angelica and bake in a very hot oven 230°C/450°F/gas mark 8 for 2 minutes until meringue is just turning golden. Serve immediately.

 Preparation time: 5 mins
Cooking time: 2 mins

RHUBARB AND CUSTARD CHARLOTTE

Serves 4–5	Metric	Imperial	American
Butter, melted	25 g	1 oz	2 tbsp
Slices bread and butter	4	4	4
Individual carton custard	1	1	1
Can rhubarb, drained reserving juice	550 g	1 lb $1/4$ oz	1 lb $1/4$ oz
Demerara (light brown) sugar	30 ml	2 tbsp	2 tbsp

1. Grease a 1.2 L/2 pt/5 cup ovenproof dish with half the melted butter.

2. Line dish with 2½ slices of the bread.

3. Spread custard in base then top with drained fruit.

4. Dice remaining bread, toss in melted butter and sugar and spoon over.

5. Bake in a hot oven 200°C/400°F/gas mark 6 for about 40 minutes until golden. Serve with reserved juice.

Preparation time: 5 mins
Cooking time: 40 mins

PINEAPPLE FLOATING ISLANDS

Use all milk instead of a mixture of milk and cream if you prefer.

Serves 4	Metric	Imperial	American
Butter	*50 g*	*2 oz*	*¼ cup*
Caster (superfine) sugar	*100 g*	*4 oz*	*½ cup*
Cornflour (cornstarch)	*25 g*	*1 oz*	*¼ cup*
Milk	*300 ml*	*½ pt*	*1¼ cups*
Single (light) cream	*150 ml*	*¼ pt*	*⅔ cup*
Can crushed pineapple, drained reserving juice	*440 g*	*15 ½ oz*	*15 ½ oz*
Eggs (size 1), separated	*4*	*4*	*4*

1. Beat butter and 50 g/2 oz/¼ cup of the sugar until light and fluffy and blend in the cornflour.

2. Warm the milk and cream but do not boil. Pour onto creamed mixture. Return to pan and cook, stirring until thickened.

3. Put crushed pineapple in base of a 1.5 L/2½ pt/6 cup ovenproof dish. Pour custard over.

4. Whisk egg whites until stiff, add 40 g/1½ oz/3 tbsp of the sugar and whisk again until glossy. Put 4 spoons full of meringue on top of the custard to make the "Island" and sprinkle with remaining sugar.

5. Bake in a slow oven 150°C/300°F/gas mark 2 for 30 minutes or until meringues are light and golden. Serve hot or cold with the reserved pineapple juice.

Preparation time: 8 mins
Cooking time: 30 mins

CHOCOLATE LEMON FLAN

Serves 4–6	Metric	Imperial	American
Chocolate digestives (graham crackers), crushed	225 g	8 oz	2 cups
Butter, melted	100 g	4 oz	½ cup
Double (heavy) or whipping cream	150 ml	¼ pt	⅔ cup
Can sweetened condensed milk	200 g	7 oz	7 oz
Lemon juice	90 ml	6 tbsp	6 tbsp
To decorate:			
Grated chocolate			

1. Mix biscuit crumbs with the butter and press into the base and sides of a 20 cm/8 in flan dish (pie pan). Chill until firm.

2. Whip cream until softly peaking. Fold in condensed milk and lemon juice. Turn into flan case. Chill, preferably overnight, then decorate with grated chocolate before serving.

 Preparation time: 5 mins plus chilling time

BLACKCURRANT MOUSSE

Serves 4	Metric	Imperial	American
Blackcurrant flavour jelly (jello) tablet	*1*	*1*	*1*
Can blackcurrants	*300 g*	*11 oz*	*11 oz*
Can evaporated milk, chilled	*175 g*	*6 oz*	*6 oz*
To decorate:			
Whipped cream			

1. Dissolve jelly in 150 ml/¹/₄ pt/²/₃ cup boiling water.

2. Stir in juice from can of blackcurrants and chill until on the point of setting.

3. Meanwhile whisk evaporated milk until thick and fluffy. When jelly is the consistency of egg white, whisk in the milk.

4. Pour into 4 glasses and chill until set. Top with whipped cream then scatter the blackcurrants over.

 Preparation time: 15 mins plus setting time

Pineapple Upside Down Pudding

Serves 6	Metric	Imperial	American
Butter	*15 g*	*½ oz*	*1 tbsp*
Demerara (light brown) sugar	*30 ml*	*2 tbsp*	*2 tbsp*
Can pineapple slices, drained reserving juice	*225 g*	*8 oz*	*8 oz*
Glacé (candied) cherries, halved			
Angelica 'leaves'			
Packet sponge cake mix	*1*	*1*	*1*
Egg and water according to packet			

1. Liberally butter a 20 cm/8 in round sandwich tin (pan) or other ovenproof dish.

2. Sprinkle sugar over base then top with pineapple rings.

3. Place a halved glacé cherry, cut side up, in centre of each ring and in gaps around. Decorate with angelica leaves in gaps.

4. Make up sponge mixture according to packet directions. Spoon over fruit.

5. Bake in a moderately hot oven 190°C/375°F/gas mark 5 for 20 minutes until risen, and centre springs back when pressed.

6. Leave to cool slightly in tin, then loosen edges and turn out onto a serving plate. Serve with the juice.

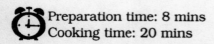 Preparation time: 8 mins
Cooking time: 20 mins

NO FUSS BAKEWELL TART

Not quite as good as a traditional one from Bakewell, but an excellent sweet all the same!

Serves 6	Metric	Imperial	American
Shortcrust pastry (basic pie crust)	*175 g*	*6 oz*	*¹/₃ lb*
Raspberry jam (conserve)	*30-45 ml*	*2-3 tbsp*	*2-3 tbsp*
Packet sponge cake mix	*1*	*1*	*1*
Egg and water as directed on packet			
Almond essence (extract)			
Flaked almonds			

1. Roll out pastry and use to line a 20 cm/8 in flan dish (pie pan) set on a baking sheet.

2. Spread jam over base.

3. Make up sponge according to packet directions. Add a few drops of almond essence. Spread over jam. Scatter with almonds.

4. Bake for 20-30 minutes at 190°F/375°F/gas mark 5 until pastry is cooked and sponge springs back when pressed. Serve warm or cold.

 Preparation time: 8 mins
Cooking time: 20-30 mins

CRÊPES SUZETTE

Serves 4	Metric	Imperial	American
Packet batter mix (made into 8 pancakes as directed)	*1*	*1*	*1*
Butter	*25 g*	*1 oz*	*2 tbsp*
Demerara (light brown) sugar	*45 ml*	*3 tbsp*	*3 tbsp*
Orange juice	*60 ml*	*4 tbsp*	*4 tbsp*
Lemon juice	*15 ml*	*1 tbsp*	*1 tbsp*
Orange liqueur or brandy	*45 ml*	*3 tbsp*	*3 tbsp*

1. Melt butter in a large frying pan (skillet). Add sugar and stir over a gentle heat until sugar dissolves.

2. Add fruit juices. Stir well to dissolve caramel (about 3-4 minutes).

3. Fold pancakes into quarters. Place one in pan, spoon over juices then push to one side. Continue until all pancakes are in the pan and bathed in juices.

4. Pour over liqueur or brandy, set alight straight away and shake pan until flames subside. Serve hot.

 Preparation time: 7 mins plus pancake cooking time

SURPRISE CHERRY PANCAKES

A variation on Crêpes Suzette for cherry fans.

Serves 4	Metric	Imperial	American
Packet batter mix (made into 8 pancakes as directed)	*1*	*1*	*1*
Low fat soft cheese	*200 g*	*7 oz*	*scant 1 cup*
Can cherry pie filling	*425 g*	*15 oz*	*15 oz*
Water	*30 ml*	*2 tbsp*	*2 tbsp*
Lemon juice	*15 ml*	*1 tbsp*	*1 tbsp*
Cherry brandy or kirsch	*45 ml*	*3 tbsp*	*3 tbsp*

1. Spread each pancake with a little of the cream cheese and fold in quarters.

2. Heat pie filling, water and lemon juice in a large frying pan (skillet). When bubbling add pancakes one at a time, bathing each in sauce and pushing it to one side before adding the next.

3. Pour over cherry brandy or kirsch. Set alight straight away and shake pan until flames subside. Serve immediately.

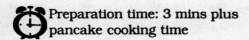 Preparation time: 3 mins plus pancake cooking time

PEAR AND CHOCOLATE ROLLS

Serves 6	Metric	Imperial	American
Filling:			
Can pears, drained			
reserving juice	*410 g*	*14¹/₂ oz*	*14¹/₂ oz*
Chocolate chips	*50 g*	*2 oz*	*¹/₂ cup*
Filo pastry sheets	*6*	*6*	*6*
Melted butter			
Sauce:			
Cocoa (unsweetened			
chocolate) powder	*15 ml*	*1 tbsp*	*1 tbsp*
Cornflour (cornstarch)	*15 ml*	*1 tbsp*	*1 tbsp*
Sugar to taste			

1. Chop pears and mix with chocolate chips.

2. Lay a filo sheet on a board. Brush with a little melted butter. Fold in half and brush lightly again.

3. Spoon a sixth of pear mixture along centre of one long edge. Fold in side edges then roll up. Place on a buttered baking sheet. Brush lightly with butter again.

4. Repeat with remaining pastry and filling.

5. Bake in a hot oven 200°C/400°F/gas mark 6 for about 15 minutes or until golden.

6. Meanwhile make sauce. Make reserved pear juice up to 300 ml/½ pt/1¼ cups with water. Blend a little with cocoa and cornflour in a saucepan. Stir in remainder. Bring to the boil and cook for 2 minutes until thickened. Sweeten to taste with sugar.

7. Serve rolls hot with a little of the chocolate sauce spooned over.

Preparation time: 15 mins
Cooking time: 15 mins

PEAR AND CINNAMON CLAFOUTIE

Serves 4–6	Metric	Imperial	American
Can pears, drained reserving juice	410 g	14¹/₂ oz	14¹/₂ oz
Butter for greasing			
Packet batter mix	1	1	1
Egg (according to packet)	1	1	1
Milk or water according to packet	300 ml	¹/₂ pt	1¹/₄ cups
Cinnamon	5 ml	1 tsp	1 tsp
Icing (confectioners') sugar for dusting			

1. Lay pears in a buttered shallow ovenproof dish.

2. Make up batter according to packet directions. Pour over. Sprinkle with cinnamon.

3. Bake in a hot oven 200°C/400°F/gas mark 6 for about 30 minutes until risen and golden. Dust with sifted icing sugar before serving with the juice.

Preparation time: 6 mins
Cooking time: about 30 mins

SPEEDY STRAWBERRY CHEESECAKE

Ring the changes with other pie fillings for toppings.

Serves 6	Metric	Imperial	American
Medium sponge flan case (pie shell)	*23 cm*	*9 in*	*9 in*
Low fat soft cheese	*200 g*	*7 oz*	*scant 1 cup*
Caster (superfine) sugar	*50 g*	*2 oz*	*¼ cup*
Vanilla essence (extract)	*2. 5 ml*	*½ tsp*	*½ tsp*
Whipped cream	*150 ml*	*¼ pt*	*⅔ cup*
Can strawberry pie filling	*425 g*	*15 oz*	*15 oz*

1.   Put flan case on a serving plate.

2.   Beat cheese with sugar and vanilla, then fold in whipped cream.

3.   Spoon into flan case and spread evenly. Chill until fairly firm.

4.   Spread pie filling over and if time chill again before serving.

 Preparation time: 3 mins plus chilling time

Snacks and Light Meals

Is grabbing a quick bite to eat because time is short the story of your life? Just because you don't want a full-blown meal, doesn't mean the food can't be tasty and satisfying. Try slitting open some pitta breads, spreading the inside with brown sauce and filling with hot baked beans before sprinkling with grated cheese and warming under the grill or the microwave. Now read on...

PIZZA ROLLS

Serves 4	Metric	Imperial	American
Soft rolls	*4*	*4*	*4*
Can chopped tomatoes,			
drained	*225 g*	*8 oz*	*8 oz*
Dried oregano	*5 ml*	*1 tsp*	*1 tsp*
Mozzarella or Cheddar			
cheese, grated			

1. Cut a slit in top of each roll, not quite through.

2. Gently pull away some of the soft filling to leave a thick shell.

3. Divide drained tomatoes between rolls. Sprinkle with herbs and top with cheese.

4. Wrap each roll in foil and steam in a steamer or colander over a saucepan of boiling water for 10 minutes until cheese has melted. Alternatively, bake in a hot oven 220°C/425°F/gas mark 7 for 10 minutes.

Note:

You can heat these Pizza Rolls in the microwave. Put in a microwave-safe dish with a lid. Do not wrap in foil. Microwave for 2 minutes, rearrange, cook a little longer depending on power output of your model. DO NOT OVERCOOK or they will be tough.

Preparation time: 3 mins
Cooking time: 10 mins

QUICK PAN PIZZA

Serves 1–2	Metric	Imperial	American
Base:			
Self-raising (self-rising) flour	100 g	4 oz	1 cup
Salt	pinch	pinch	pinch
Oil	45 ml	3 tbsp	3 tbsp
Water to mix			
Topping:			
Can chopped tomatoes, drained	225 g	8 oz	8 oz
Dried oregano	1.5 ml	1/4 tsp	1/4 tsp
Cheddar or Mozzarella cheese, grated	50 g	2 oz	1/2 cup
Additional toppings suggestions: chopped ham, sliced mushrooms, drained sweetcorn (corn), diced (bell) pepper, pepperoni, drained pineapple pieces			

1. Mix flour with salt and 30 ml/2 tbsp of the oil in a bowl. Add enough cold water to form a soft but not sticky dough.

2. Knead gently then flatten out to a round to fit base of frying pan (skillet).

3. Heat remaining oil in pan, add base and fry (sauté) for about 3 minutes until golden underneath. Turn over.

4. Spread tomatoes over, sprinkle with herbs (add any other topping of choice) then sprinkle with cheese.

5. Fry for 2-3 minutes then place pan under a hot grill (broiler) and cook until cheese is melted and bubbling. Serve hot.

Preparation time: 5 mins
Cooking time: 7 mins

CONVENIENT CROQUE MADAME

Serves 1	Metric	Imperial	American
Bread slices	2	2	2
Butter			
Processed cheese slice	1	1	1
Onion sliced and separated into rings	1	1	1
Dried sage	1.5 ml	1/4 tsp	1/4 tsp

1.   Butter bread. Sandwich together with cheese, onion rings and sage, buttered sides out.

2.   Fry (sauté) on each side for about 2 minutes or until golden and cheese has melted. Serve immediately.

Preparation time: 2 mins
Cooking time: about 4 mins

SALMON TARTARE SANDWICHES

Makes 4 rounds	Metric	Imperial	American
Butter or margarine	75 g	3 oz	1/3 cup
Can pink salmon, drained	100 g	4 oz	4 oz
Tartare sauce	30 ml	2 tbsp	2 tbsp
Chopped parsley	15 ml	1 tbsp	1 tbsp
Salt and pepper			
Bread slices	8	8	8

1.   Put butter in a bowl and mash with a fork.

2. Discard bones and skin from fish and mash into butter with the tartare sauce, parsley and a little salt and pepper.

3. Spread over slices of bread and sandwich together in pairs. Cut crusts off if liked. Cut in triangles and serve.

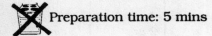 Preparation time: 5 mins

ORANGE AND CREAM CHEESE DECKERS

Makes 3 rounds	Metric	Imperial	American
Bread slices	6	6	6
Low fat soft cheese	200 g	7 oz	scant 1 cup
Can mandarin oranges, drained	300 g	11 oz	11 oz
Cress or lettuce			
Black pepper			

1. Spread bread with the cheese.

2. Top half the slices with oranges then cress or shredded lettuce leaves.

3. Season with pepper then sandwich together with remaining bread slices. Cut and serve.

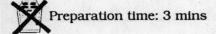 Preparation time: 3 mins

DILL SQUARES

Serves 1–2	Metric	Imperial	American
Bread slices	2	2	2
Butter			
Dill pickle, large, sliced	1	1	1
Cheddar cheese, grated	50 g	2 oz	½ cup

1. Toast bread and spread with butter.

2. Top with slices of pickle then grated cheese.

3. Place under a hot grill (broiler) until golden and bubbling. Serve hot.

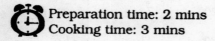 Preparation time: 2 mins
Cooking time: 3 mins

EGGY BAGUETTE

Serves 1–2	Metric	Imperial	American
Small French stick	1	1	1
Butter			
Eggs	2	2	2
Dried mixed herbs	1.5 ml	¼ tsp	¼ tsp
Salt and pepper			

1. Warm French stick either in the oven, under the grill (broiler) turning frequently or in the microwave (not too long!). Cut a slit along length and butter inside.

2. Meanwhile beat eggs and add 30 ml/2 tbsp water, the herbs and some salt and pepper. Beat well.

3. Heat an omelette pan and add a knob of butter. When sizzling, pour in egg mixture. Lift and stir egg until set. Fold in three.

4. Slide inside French stick and cut in half, if liked.

 Preparation time: 5 mins

WAFFLE DAGWOODS

Serves 2	Metric	Imperial	American
Frozen potato waffles	4	4	4
Eggs	2	2	2
Butter or oil			
Ham slices	2	2	2
Lettuce, shredded			

1. Grill (broil) or fry (sauté) waffles according to packet directions.

2. Fry (sauté) eggs in a little butter or oil until cooked.

3. Place a slice of ham on 2 waffles. Top each with an egg and some shredded lettuce. Top with second waffle and try to eat!

Preparation time: 2 mins
Cooking time: about 6 mins

FISH FINGERS AMERICAN-STYLE

Serves 2	Metric	Imperial	American
Fish fingers	8	8	8
Soft baps	2	2	2
Processed cheese slices	2	2	2
Tartare sauce	30 ml	2 tbsp	2 tbsp
Lettuce, shredded			

1. Grill (broil), fry (sauté) or microwave fish fingers.

2. Split rolls and lay 4 fish fingers in each roll.

3. Top with a slice of cheese and flash under a hot grill (broiler) to melt cheese.

4. Top with tartare sauce, shredded lettuce and then lid of roll. Serve.

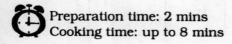 Preparation time: 2 mins
Cooking time: up to 8 mins

PLOUGHMAN'S GRILL

Serves 1–2	Metric	Imperial	American
Bread slices	2	2	2
Butter	25 g	1 oz	2 tbsp
Cheddar cheese, grated	50 g	2 oz	1/2 cup
Pickled onions, chopped	2	2	2

1. Toast bread on both sides.

2. Meanwhile, mash butter with the cheese and pickled onions.

3. Spread over toast and grill (broil) until golden and bubbling. Serve hot.

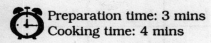 Preparation time: 3 mins
Cooking time: 4 mins

PITTA POCKETS

Serves 1	Metric	Imperial	American
Pitta bread	*1*	*1*	*1*
Lettuce, shredded	*15 ml*	*1 tbsp*	*1 tbsp*
Tomato slices	*2*	*2*	*2*
Cucumber slices	*2*	*2*	*2*
Filling suggestion:			
Tuna, chopped ham, mashed pilchard, sliced corned beef, chopped frankfurter, salami or hard-boiled (hard-cooked) egg	*15 ml*	*1 tbsp*	*1 tbsp*
Mayonnaise	*10 ml*	*2 tsp*	*2 tsp*

1. Toast or microwave pitta just to heat through enough to puff up. Split along one long edge to form a pocket.

2. Add shredded lettuce, tomato, cucumber and either tuna or other suggested filling. Finish with mayonnaise.

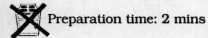 Preparation time: 2 mins

CHEESE AND MUSHROOM CROISSANTS

If you buy ready split croissants, they can be used straight from the freezer.

Serves 2–4	Metric	Imperial	American
Croissants	*4*	*4*	*4*
Can creamed mushrooms	*215 g*	*7¹/₂ oz*	*7¹/₂ oz*
Cheddar cheese, grated	*50 g*	*2 oz*	*¹/₂ cup*

1. Carefully open croissants where split is, without breaking apart. Or make a slit in each if necessary.

2. Spread creamed mushrooms inside and pack in cheese.

3. Grill (broil) until cheese has melted, turning once, and croissants are crisp and hot through. Take care not to burn. Alternatively heat as for Pizza Rolls (page 153). Serve.

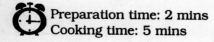 Preparation time: 2 mins
Cooking time: 5 mins

NAN TIFFIN

Serves 4	Metric	Imperial	American
Nan breads	2	2	2
Can pease pudding	225 g	8 oz	8 oz
Curry paste	10 ml	2 tsp	2 tsp
Mango chutney	30 ml	2 tbsp	2 tbsp
Lemon juice			
Lettuce, shredded (optional)			

1. Grill or microwave nans according to packet directions.

2. Heat pease pudding with the curry paste in a saucepan or the microwave until hot through, stirring occasionally.

3. Spread pease pudding mixture over surface of nans.

4. Spread mango chutney over and sprinkle on lemon juice. Add shredded lettuce, if liked.

5. Fold in halves, then cut into handy sized wedges.

6. Wrap in kitchen paper and eat in the fingers.

Preparation time: 2 mins
Cooking time: 3 mins

TEATIME TREATS

We tend to think that tea-time as a meal with cups of tea, bread, jam, cakes and biscuits is a thing of the past. Yet how many of us love a little something with our mid-afternoon cuppa? When we have guests to lunch on Sundays, it still seems appropriate to provide a snack at tea-time and, as I seldom think about it in advance, it's got to be something quick knocked up from the storecupboard!

NO-BAKE CRUNCHY BARS

These are ideal for lunch boxes too.

Makes 12–16	Metric	Imperial	American
Butter or margarine	175 g	6 oz	³/₄ cup
Soft brown sugar	50 g	2 oz	¹/₄ cup
Golden (light corn) syrup	30 ml	2 tbsp	2 tbsp
Cocoa (unsweetened chocolate) powder	45 ml	3 tbsp	3 tbsp
Raisins	75 g	3 oz	¹/₂ cup
Original Oat Crunch cereal	350 g	12 oz	3 cups
Plain (semi-sweet) chocolate	225 g	8 oz	2 cups

1. Oil and line base of an 18 x 28 cm/7 x 11 in baking tin (pan) with baking parchment.

2. Melt butter or margarine, sugar, syrup and cocoa in a pan. Stir in raisins and cereal. Press into tin.

3. Melt chocolate in a pan over hot water or in a microwave and spread over right to the corners.

4. Chill until set, cut into fingers and store in an airtight tin.

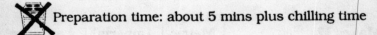 Preparation time: about 5 mins plus chilling time

QUICK RUM TRUFFLES

Makes 12	Metric	Imperial	American
Chocolate hazelnut spread	*30 ml*	*2 tbsp*	*2 tbsp*
Cake crumbs	*50 g*	*2 oz*	*1 cup*
Rum, brandy or sherry			
essence (extract)	*5 ml*	*1 tsp*	*1 tsp*
Water			
Cocoa (unsweetened			
chocolate) powder,			
drinking chocolate			
powder or chocolate			
vermicelli to coat			

1. Mix chocolate spread and cake crumbs together until well blended.

2. Add essence to taste and a little water to give a soft, but not sticky consistency.

3. Roll mixture into small balls then roll in cocoa or vermicelli. Place in small paper cases and chill.

Preparation time: 10 mins plus chilling time

THE EASIEST FLAPJACKS

Makes 12	Metric	Imperial	American
Butter or margarine,			
softened	*75 g*	*3 oz*	*¹/₃ cup*
Demerara (light brown)			
sugar	*75 g*	*3 oz*	*¹/₃ cup*
Rolled oats	*100 g*	*4 oz*	*1 cup*
Mixed (apple pie) spice			
(optional)	*5 ml*	*1 tsp*	*1 tsp*

1. Beat butter or margarine in a bowl until creamy.

2. Add sugar, oats and spice, if using, and work in until well mixed.

3. Turn into a greased 18 cm/7 in square tin and press down well. Bake in a hot oven 220°C/425°F/gas mark 7 for 15-20 minutes until golden.

4. Leave to cool in tin for 10 minutes then cut into pieces. Leave in tin until cold before removing.

Preparation time: 3 mins
Cooking time: 15-20 mins

FRESH CREAM GÂTEAU

Serves 6–8	Metric	Imperial	American
Packet sponge cake mix	*1*	*1*	*1*
Egg (according to packet)	*1*	*1*	*1*
Raspberry jam (conserve)	*30 ml*	*2 tbsp*	*2 tbsp*
Whipping cream	*150 ml*	*¼ pt*	*⅔ cup*
Icing (confectioners') sugar for dusting			

1. Make up cake mix according to packet directions. Divide between two sandwich tins and bake as directed.

2. Turn out onto a wire rack to cool.

3. Sandwich cakes together with the jam and whipped cream. Dust top with icing sugar and chill until ready to serve.

Preparation time: 5 mins
Cooking time: 20 mins plus cooling time

CINNAMON FRENCH TOAST

Serves 4	Metric	Imperial	American
Egg	1	1	1
Milk	30 ml	2 tbsp	2 tbsp
Thick slices white bread, crusts removed	4	4	4
Butter	25 g	1 oz	2 tbsp
Oil	30 ml	2 tbsp	2 tbsp
Caster (superfine) sugar	20 ml	4 tsp	4 tsp
Cinnamon	5 ml	1 tsp	1 tsp

1. Beat egg and milk together. Dip bread in to coat completely.

2. Heat butter and oil in a large frying pan (skillet). Fry (sauté) slices for about 1½ minutes over a high heat until a deep golden brown.

3. Drain on kitchen paper.

4. Mix sugar and cinnamon on a flat plate. Dip the bread in mixture until coated on both sides. Serve straight away cut into triangles.

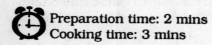 Preparation time: 2 mins
Cooking time: 3 mins

CHEWY APRICOT BARS

Makes 15	Metric	Imperial	American
Can evaporated milk	175 g	6 oz	6 oz
Clear honey	20 ml	4 tsp	4 tsp
Apple juice	45 ml	3 tbsp	3 tbsp
Butter	50 g	2 oz	1/4 cup
Soft brown sugar	50 g	2 oz	1/4 cup
Sultanas (golden raisins)	50 g	2 oz	1/3 cup
Raisins	50 g	2 oz	1/3 cup
Ready-to-eat dried apricots, chopped	225 g	8 oz	1 1/3 cups
Desiccated (shredded) coconut	100 g	4 oz	1 cup
Rolled oats	225 g	8 oz	2 cups

1. Grease a 28 x 18 cm/11 x 7 in baking tin (pan).

2. Heat evaporated milk with the honey, apple juice, butter and sugar until melted.

3. Add remaining ingredients and mix well. Press into tin.

4. Wrap in cling film (plastic wrap) and chill overnight to allow flavours to develop before cutting into bars.

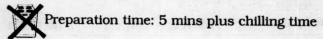 Preparation time: 5 mins plus chilling time

FRUIT AND FIBRE CRACKLES

Makes 15	Metric	Imperial	American
Plain (semi-sweet) chocolate	100 g	4 oz	1 cup
Butter or margarine	50 g	2 oz	1/4 cup
Golden (light-corn) syrup	15 ml	1 tbsp	1 tbsp
Fruit and Fibre breakfast cereal	100 g	4 oz	2 cups

1. Melt chocolate in a bowl over a pan of hot water or in the microwave.

2. Beat in the butter or margarine and syrup until smooth, heating a little more if necessary.

3. Stir in the cereal. Pack into paper cases and chill until firm.

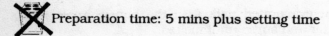 Preparation time: 5 mins plus setting time

PEANUT BITES

Makes 18	Metric	Imperial	American
Plain biscuits (cookies), crushed	225 g	8 oz	2 cups
Butter, melted	100 g	4 oz	1/2 cup
Crunchy peanut butter	225 g	8 oz	1 cup
Glacé (candied) cherries, chopped	25 g	1 oz	2 tbsp
Currants	25 g	1 oz	2 tbsp

1. Mix all ingredients together until well blended.

2. Press into a greased 28 x 18 cm/11 x 7 in baking tin (pan). Cover with foil or cling film (plastic wrap) and chill until firm before cutting into squares.

 Preparation time: 4 mins plus chilling time

RASPBERRY OAT SQUARES

Makes 15	Metric	Imperial	American
Self-raising (self-rising) flour	*225 g*	*8 oz*	*2 cups*
Salt	*5 ml*	*1 tsp*	*1 tsp*
Margarine	*175 g*	*6 oz*	*3/4 cup*
Rolled oats	*175 g*	*6 oz*	*1 1/2 cups*
Caster (superfine) sugar	*175 g*	*6 oz*	*3/4 cup*
Can raspberries	*300 g*	*11 oz*	*11 oz*

1. Put flour and salt in a bowl. Rub in the margarine, then stir in the oats and sugar.

2. Grease a 28 x 18 cm/11 x 7 in baking tin (pan) and press half the mixture into base.

3. Drain raspberries and scatter fruit over the top.

4. Cover with remaining crumble mixture, pressing down well.

5. Bake in a hot oven 200°C/400°F/gas mark 6 for 30 minutes. Leave to cool for 15 minutes then cut into squares and transfer to a wire rack to cool completely.

Preparation time: 8 mins
Cooking time: 30 mins plus cooling time

BROKEN BISCUIT CAKES

You can buy packets of broken biscuits very cheaply or use up the dregs of the biscuit barrel.

Makes 15	Metric	Imperial	American
Butter or margarine	*100 g*	*4 oz*	*½ cup*
Caster (superfine) sugar	*15 ml*	*1 tbsp*	*1 tbsp*
Golden (light corn) syrup	*15 ml*	*1 tbsp*	*1 tbsp*
Cocoa (unsweetened chocolate) powder	*30 ml*	*2 tbsp*	*2 tbsp*
Broken biscuits (cookies), crushed	*225 g*	*8 oz*	*2 cups*
Sultanas (golden raisins)	*50 g*	*2 oz*	*⅓ cup*

1. Melt the fat, sugar, syrup and cocoa in a saucepan until well blended, but do not boil.

2. Stir in the biscuits and sultanas.

3. Press into a greased 28 x 18 cm/11 x 7 in baking tin (pan). Chill until firm then cut into squares.

 Preparation time: 3 mins
Cooking time: 2 mins plus chilling time

SAUCES & SAVOURY BUTTERS

Sauces and savoury butters can spike up plain chops or fish fillets from your freezer or brighten a basically boring can of anything from tuna to frankfurters.

QUICK TOMATO SAUCE

Use for everything from pasta to pork chops. When you're in a desperate hurry, just use passata straight from the jar, seasoned, if you like, with a little garlic purée, granules or the real thing, and a pinch of dried oregano.

Serves 4	Metric	Imperial	American
Onion, chopped	*1*	*1*	*1*
Oil	*15 ml*	*1 tbsp*	*1 tbsp*
Can chopped tomatoes	*400 g*	*14 oz*	*14 oz*
Tomato purée (paste)	*15 ml*	*1 tbsp*	*1 tbsp*
Salt and pepper			
Dried oregano	*2.5 ml*	*¹/₂ tsp*	*¹/₂ tsp*

1. Fry (sauté) onion in the oil for 2 minutes to soften.

2. Add remaining ingredients, bring to the boil and simmer for 10 minutes until pulpy. Use as required.

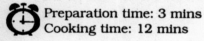 Preparation time: 3 mins
Cooking time: 12 mins

ALL-PURPOSE BARBECUE SAUCE

Use as a side sauce with grills or barbecues, or as cooking sauce for chops, chicken or fish.

Serves 4	Metric	Imperial	American
Lemon juice	*15 ml*	*1 tbsp*	*1 tbsp*
Red wine (or other) vinegar	*15 ml*	*1 tbsp*	*1 tbsp*
Tomato ketchup (catsup)	*30 ml*	*2 tbsp*	*2 tbsp*
Worcestershire sauce	*15 ml*	*1 tbsp*	*1 tbsp*
Golden (light corn) syrup	*30 ml*	*2 tbsp*	*2 tbsp*

1. Mix all ingredients together until thoroughly blended.

2. Store in a screw-topped jar in the fridge for up to 1 month.

 Preparation time: 3 mins

GARLIC AND HERB SAUCE

Serve with fish, vegetables or white meat.

Serves 4	Metric	Imperial	American
Cornflour (cornstarch)	15 ml	1 tbsp	1 tbsp
Milk	300 ml	1/2 pt	1 1/4 cups
Butter or margarine	15 g	1/2 oz	1 tbsp
Garlic and herb cheese	90 g	3 1/2 oz	1/2 cup
Salt and pepper			

1. Whisk cornflour with a little of the milk in a saucepan until smooth. Stir in remaining milk. Add butter or margarine.

2. Bring to the boil, stirring until thickened.

3. Add cheese cut into pieces and continue stirring over a gentle heat until blended. Season with salt and pepper and use as required.

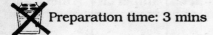 Preparation time: 2 mins
Cooking time: 4 mins

Gran's Salad Dressing

Use as an alternative to mayonnaise for everything from coleslaw to beetroot.

Serves 4–6	Metric	Imperial	American
Demerara (light brown) sugar	15 ml	1 tbsp	1 tbsp
English mustard, made	5 ml	1 tsp	1 tsp
Single (light) cream (or evaporated milk)	150 ml	¼ pt	⅔ cup
Malt vinegar			
Salt and pepper			

1. Mix sugar, mustard and cream or evaporated milk together until sugar dissolves.

2. Whisk in vinegar to taste. Season with salt and pepper. Store in a screw-topped jar in the refrigerator for up to 2 weeks.

Preparation time: 3 mins

Cocktail Sauce

Use to brighten up cold fish, chicken or vegetables or serve as a dip.

Serves 4	Metric	Imperial	American
Mayonnaise	60 ml	4 tbsp	4 tbsp
Plain yoghurt or single (light) cream	30 ml	2 tbsp	2 tbsp
Tomato ketchup (catsup)	15 ml	1 tbsp	1 tbsp
Horseradish cream	10 ml	2 tsp	2 tsp
Salt and pepper			

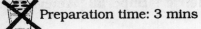

1. Blend all ingredients together until smooth.

2. Store in a screw-topped jar in the fridge for up to 1 week. Use as required.

 Preparation time: 3 mins

STROGANOFF SAUCE

Use with stir-fry meats or fillets of fish.

Serves 4	Metric	Imperial	American
Onion, finely chopped	*1*	*1*	*1*
Butter	*15 g*	*½ oz*	*1 tbsp*
Brandy	*15 ml*	*1 tbsp*	*1 tbsp*
Cornflour (cornstarch)	*20 ml*	*4 tsp*	*4 tsp*
Milk	*300 ml*	*½ pt*	*1¼ cups*
Soft cheese with black pepper	*90 g*	*3½ oz*	*½ cup*
Salt			
Chopped parsley	*15 ml*	*1 tbsp*	*1 tbsp*

1. Fry (sauté) onion in the butter gently for 3 minutes until soft, not brown.

2. Blend brandy with the cornflour and a little of the milk. Stir in remaining milk and add to pan. Bring to the boil, stirring until thickened.

3. Add cheese in small pieces and continue stirring over a gentle heat until blended. Season with salt. Add parsley. Use as required.

Preparation time: 2 mins
Cooking time: 6 mins

GARLIC BUTTER

Serves 4 (or enough for 1 small French stick)	Metric	Imperial	American
Garlic clove, crushed or garlic purée (paste)	1	1	1
or granules	5 ml	1 tsp	1 tsp
Butter, softened	75 g	3 oz	1/3 cup
Black pepper			

1. Mash garlic into the butter and add a good grinding of pepper. Either spread in French bread (or rolls), wrap in foil and bake until crisp and melted OR

2. Shape into a roll on a piece of baking parchment, roll up and chill ready to cut in slices to top plain cooked meat or fish.

Variations:

* Garlic and Herb: Add 5 ml/1 tsp dried mixed herbs to garlic butter above.

* Herb: Omit garlic and add 10 ml/2 tsp dried mixed herbs to plain butter and continue as above.

* Tomato: Add 15 ml/1 tbsp tomato purée (paste) to plain or garlic butter. Mash thoroughly to mix. Continue as above.

* Anchovy Butter: Add 10 ml/2 tsp anchovy essence (extract) to plain butter, continue as above.

* Curry butter: Add 5 ml/1 tsp (or to taste) curry paste to plain or garlic butter. Mash thoroughly to mix. Continue as above.

 Preparation time: 2 mins plus chilling time

Index